the Homework Handbook

Practical Advice You Can Use Tonight to Help Your Child Succeed Tomorrow

**Harriett Cholden, M.Ed., and John Friedman, Ph.D.
with Ethel Tiersky, M.A.**

CB
CONTEMPORARY BOOKS

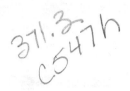

Library of Congress Cataloging-in-Publication Data

Cholden, Harriett.
    The homework handbook : practical advice you can use tonight to help your child
succeed tomorrow / Harriett Cholden, John A. Friedman, and Ethel Tiersky.
        p.   cm.
    Includes bibliographical references (p.).
    ISBN 0-8092-2881-5
    1. Homework—Handbooks, manuals, etc. 2. Education—Parent participation—
Handbooks, manuals, etc.   I. Friedman, John A.   II. Tiersky, Ethel, 1937-   .   III
Title.
LB1048.C47   1998
371.3′028′1—dc21   98-6083
                                                                                        CIP

Cartoon on page 4 reprinted with special permission of King Features Syndicate.
Cartoon on page 133 reprinted by permission of United Feature Syndicate, Inc.

Cover design by Monica Baziuk
Interior design by Jeanette Wojtyla

Published by Contemporary Books
A division of NTC/Contemporary Publishing Group, Inc.
4255 West Touhy Avenue, Lincolnwood (Chicago), Illinois 60646-1975 U.S.A.
Printed in the United States of America
International Standard Book Number: 0-8092-2881-5
18   17   16   15   14   13   12   11   10   9   8   7   6   5   4   3   2   1

To our spouses:
Myron Cholden, Brenda Friedman, and Martin Tiersky

And to our children:
Nicholas Friedman, Andrew Friedman, Howard and Lana Tiersky,
Arthur Tiersky, and Marcia Tiersky

in gratitude for their input, encouragement, and invaluable support,
without which this project would have been impossible

Contents

About the Authors

Harriett Cholden has been teaching at the Francis W. Parker School in Chicago since 1963. Her articles about teaching have appeared in numerous popular and professional journals. Her innovative and effective techniques have helped hundreds of parents and students solve their homework problems. In recent years Mrs. Cholden and coauthor Dr. John Friedman have shared their homework strategies by lecturing to parent groups, appearing on television and radio, and writing articles. They have also been the subject of newspaper features in the United States and Scotland.

John Friedman, a Chicago-area psychologist, specializes in child and family therapy and frequently deals with homework problems. He is on the staff of Northwestern University Medical School's Department of Psychiatry, and his writings have appeared in numerous professional journals and books.

Ethel Tiersky teaches English at Harry S. Truman College in Chicago. She is a prolific freelance writer and the mother of three grown children, who have helped her to become intimately acquainted with homework hassles.

Preface

Homework avoidance, homework frustration, and homework anxiety. Student ailments? Yes. But they also plague parents. Misunderstanding of assignments, inadequate time management, competition from television, sports, and family obligations are frequent homework hurdles. Whether problems originate with the student, teacher, or parent, the student's response is often played out in self-defeating attitudes and habits.

During my thirty-five-year teaching odyssey, I have regularly encountered homework crises. To help students and parents cope with them, I developed effective strategies to reframe stubborn homework and study problems. These solutions were guided by the research of other educators and my own experimentation.

I met Dr. John Friedman, a child psychologist, at a student staffing (my student, his patient). We found that we shared many beliefs about ways to help youngsters resolve their homework problems. One important component we agreed upon was the need for a partnership between pupil, parent, and teacher. Incentives for the student to succeed were another necessary component—not punishment, parent control, or a hierarchy with the student at the bottom of the ladder. The student's voice had to be heard.

Subsequently, Dr. Friedman and I wrote an article, "Whose Homework Is It, Anyway?" As a result, we were invited to lecture at various parent forums throughout the Chicago area. Although our audiences were from diverse socioeconomic communities, inner city to affluent suburbs, parents are parents and kids are kids, so the questions could not have been more similar. Basically, parents wanted to know how much and how best to help their children with homework. Our experiences at these meetings demonstrated the need to answer parental concerns from both of our perspectives, teacher and therapist. We invited Ethel Tiersky, a college teacher and professional writer, to help us bring current thought and our own methods and ideas to you.

In the preparation of this manuscript, we received support, encouragement, and inspiration from all facets of the Francis W. Parker School community including my nearly one thousand fifth-grade students (whom I've taught over the years), their parents (clearly too many to name, although I would like to, and they deserve it), my fellow teachers, the Parker administrators, and others who took the time to answer our questionnaires.

Valuable insights were gained from those whom I interviewed: Susan Agate, Allison Kimball, Karen Harrison, Meg Heron, Joe Ruggiero, Jacqueline Rudman, and Janet Sullivan.

Our thanks also to many others who shared their professional expertise with us: Alison Abbott, Sylvia and Joe Accardi, Ann Hills Breed, Esther Dickstein, Mary Dilg, Paul Druzinsky, Anne Duncan, Jack Ellison, Cokey Evans, Daniel Frank, Beverly Greenberg, Katie Haskins, Leah Hite, Patricia Horsch, Barbara Hunt, Rosemary Johnson, Mark Mattson, Don Monroe, Norma Nelson, Chuck Olin, Marilyn Ratliff, and Rebecca Rossof.

We're very grateful, too, for the editorial assistance provided by the following friends and relatives: Myron Cholden, Bonnie Seebold, Marie Kirchner Stone, and Martin Tiersky. Thanks also to our NTC/Contemporary Publishing Group editors, Betsy Lancefield and Craig Bolt, for their help, encouragement, and confidence in our project.

Finally, I would like to honor the memory of my first mentor and master teacher at Parker School, Lynn Pierson Martin. Her faith in my ability to make a difference in the lives of young people has been an inspiration to me during my entire career.

Harriett Cholden

INTRODUCTION

Why Homework?

As millions listened, President Clinton delivered his 1996 State of the Union Address and gave parents this urgent message: "Turn off the TV. See that the homework is done." Why would the President spotlight something as mundane as homework? Despite educational reforms, statistics about American learning remain scary enough to inspire such attention. U.S. Department of Education studies tell us that more than 40 percent of the nation's fourth-grade students cannot read at grade level, and nearly 40 percent of American eighth graders lack even basic number skills. Problems persist into high school. Since 1965 there has been a 75 percent decline in the absolute number of students scoring above 650 in verbal and math college entrance tests, says Professor E. D. Hirsch, author of *The Schools We Need and Why We Don't Have Them* (1996).

What to do about this bad news? Ideas often mentioned include a longer school day (or year), more homework, and more family involvement. But more is not always better. *Our main goal in this book is to help parents discover how to participate in their children's learning in ways that lead to a better education and more positive attitudes toward academic endeavors.*

As parents, you can become involved in two general ways. First, you can strive to improve American education one child at a time. By focusing upon the needs of your particular child, you can help put one more student in the success column. This book will tell you how to provide encouragement, assistance, and inspiration that will strengthen your child's ability to learn.

But there is a second way you can help. Get involved in your child's school. If you and your neighbors provide additional resources for the school, the school can offer more to kids. Whatever you know about—from architecture to zoology, from computers to comic strips—can be developed into a classroom presentation. If you speak a foreign language or cook for an ethnic palate, those abilities can be utilized by schools. If you have a warm, supportive way with kids, consider becoming a mentor, tutor, or volunteer classroom assistant. When you volunteer to teach other children, you teach your own children wonderful lessons about the importance of sharing knowledge and helping others. You also demonstrate the value you place upon education. The National Parent Teacher Association (PTA) urges parents to become involved in their children's education and their schools, pointing out what research confirms: family involvement increases student attendance, attitude, motivation, behavior, and achievement.

Getting back specifically to homework: just what should it accomplish? Teachers assign it with five main purposes in mind:

- to provide further practice with skills and information acquired in class
- to provide opportunities for extension and enrichment (for doing research, using knowledge in creative ways, practicing problem-solving skills, applying knowledge to new situations, integrating various skills and knowledge into one project, pursuing special interests in greater depth)
- to individualize assignments in order to meet the needs, abilities, and interests of a diverse group of students
- to complete work begun in class
- to prepare students for new classroom instruction (for example, by reading about a topic before it is introduced in class)

But the academic benefits of homework are just the tip of the iceberg. Homework teaches children so much more than facts and skills.

- Homework can be character-building. Keeping up with homework through one's own initiative means accepting responsibility, persevering when the going gets tough, resisting distractions, seeing a job through to its completion, and developing self-reliance by handling work independently.
- Homework can help children develop study habits that successful students need, such as budgeting time and organizing information.
- Homework helps children realize that learning is not just a school-based, teacher-directed activity. Homework encourages kids to become independent, self-taught, life-long learners.

Not only does homework educate kids; it also educates parents and teachers by serving as a link between home and school. Homework enables parents to become more involved in their children's learning because it shows parents what their children are studying in school, what skills to reinforce, and what family enrichment activities might tie in with school studies. And when homework assignments utilize children's experiences within the family, the product gives teachers a glimpse into the home lives of their students and an opportunity to understand them better.

Still, homework gets a lot of bad press. Kids tend to consider it a nuisance. Parents find it an additional item to worry about. To teachers it means mounds of additional papers to correct. Is it worth all the trouble? Does homework really help? Does it really lead to an increase in academic achievement? The answer is generally yes, but how much depends upon what grade level you're talking about. A U.S. Department of Education report entitled "What Works: Research about Teaching and Learning" (1986) confirms the importance of homework with the following statistics:

- When low-ability students do one to three hours of homework per week, their grades are usually as high as the grades of average students who do no homework.

• When students of average ability do three to five hours of homework per week, their grades usually equal those of high-ability students who do no homework.

An article in the British newspaper *The Economist* (May 6, 1995) surveys homework research in the United Kingdom and the United States. The studies discussed here show that children who complete moderate to heavy amounts of homework do much better academically than those who do less. It's not hard to figure out why. Homework extends the amount of time spent on schooling. As the article points out, "It provides practice, teaches discipline, and, not least important, helps focus family life and parents' attention on education." The studies surveyed in the article reached the following conclusions: (1) the power of homework to influence academic success ranks second only to ability; and (2) homework is a greater determiner of academic success than either race or family background.

Professor Harris Cooper, a University of Missouri social psychologist who has researched and written extensively about homework, states emphatically, "Every child should be doing it." In *The Battle Over Homework* (1994), Cooper agrees that homework has a positive effect upon academic achievement. Older students, he says, benefit most. The correlation between homework and achievement is very small in grades four to six, twice as large for junior high students, and twice as large again for high school students. However, this does *not* mean that homework is unimportant for younger students. In a 1998 article in the *Journal of Educational Psychology*, Cooper says that homework in early grades, when it helps youngsters develop good study habits, has a long-term positive effect upon secondary school achievement. We're convinced that there are also immediate benefits when younger students bring their studies home. Our own experience indicates that, for kids who need help with the basics of reading and math, practicing with a parent (either teacher-assigned extra work or parent-designed enrichment) can make the difference between falling behind and keeping up.

If homework is so important, are teachers assigning more and are kids doing more than in past years? That depends upon what community you're talking about. Cooper notes, with regret, the great disparity in the amount of homework assigned from one community to another. In some areas, parents send a message to teachers that they value education highly and want teachers to assign a lot of homework, and the teachers comply. In other neighborhoods, where parents are less supportive of homework, teachers may assign little or none, and these children are being cheated.

For homework to be beneficial, all three participants—student, teacher, and parent—must do their parts well. Teachers must develop interesting, appropriate assignments and provide helpful feedback on completed work; students must be committed to doing the work; and parents must be supportive without being intrusive.

Of course, homework can be detrimental if it's too much or too soon. But, when assignments are developmentally appropriate, more homework need not mean more misery for kids. It's all in one's point of view. A University of Michigan cross-cultural study (discussed in *The Economist* article previously mentioned) revealed that eleven-year-olds in Taiwan do twice as much homework as Japanese kids of the same age. And the Japanese students, in turn, do twice as much as American fifth graders. But guess who likes homework the least. Right, the Americans. And which students like it the most? The Chinese students. According to the researchers, this evidence demonstrates that "a culture devoted to education need not be one where children find studying bitter or pointless."

Twentieth-century Americans have had an on-again, off-again romance with homework as educational theories and current events have shaped attitudes. In some decades homework has been valued, in others devalued. In 1901 the state of California banned homework for children under the age of thirteen. However, in the early decades of the century, homework (mostly memorization) was generally viewed as good exercise for the mind. In *The Battle Over Homework*, Harris Cooper describes the cycles of the past fifty-some years. The 1940s brought a reaction against homework, as the value of memorization was called into question and the life-adjustment movement touted the importance of leisure time. Then came the 1950s when Russia's *Sputnik* satellite aroused American fears about falling behind in math and science; homework was called to the rescue. By the mid-1960s homework was "out" again, viewed as too great a burden upon kids. (Moreover, some progressive educators of this decade worried that homework only encouraged parents to function as amateur and inadequate teachers, to the detriment of their children.) Then came the educational reform movement of the 1980s and another homework renaissance.

Current research continues to support the idea that both homework and parents play an important role in the educational enterprise. In a study entitled "Doing Homework: Perspectives of Elementary and Junior High Students" (1994), authors Janis Bryan and Carol Nelson say, "In general, researchers have found that there is a positive correlation between homework and achievement, and between parent involvement in homework and student attitudes about school." Today, almost a century after California's homework ban, most parents, educators, and researchers have climbed aboard the homework bandwagon. Now we must take care to guide it well to help kids reach the desired destination with their confidence and enthusiasm intact. And that's what this book is all about.

1

Defining Homework Problems

In most families homework is at least an occasional headache, and in far too many households the "homework blues" is a recurring theme. Yet, so far, not a single scientist has located the obvious solution—that elusive homework gene. Every week, it seems, news media reveal another startling genetic secret—a gene that induces people to overeat, another that lures them toward a life of danger, and so on. But where, oh where, is the one parents need most? If there's a gene that attracts kids to sweets and skydiving, why not one that pulls them toward textbooks? Drop a homework gene into the hereditary packet, and—presto!—tranquility will grace the after-dinner dining room table as cheerful youngsters tackle their academic tasks with enthusiasm and intense concentration. At least, that may be a common parental fantasy.

Children, on the other hand, may conjure up another solution to homework blues: the Homework Genie. Of course, Homework Genie would be visible only to students. Rub the magic lamp, mumble the magic words, and an omniscient (and neat) homework helper (smarter even than Mom or Dad) would take over the irksome task, leaving Master free to put his energies where they belong—into Nintendo.

Nothing wrong with wishful thinking, but it's unlikely that either high-tech science or ancient magic will solve the homework problem. Parents, teachers, and kids must work it out. Of course, some lucky parents have kids that seem to have been injected with a homework gene. These kids take their homework seriously and do it diligently and accurately. But this year's Hardworking Hortense could turn into next year's Lazy Lizzie. Kids go through phases, and parents suffer through them. When problems develop, solutions often involve all three partners in the homework triangle: the parents, the student, and the teacher.

To President Clinton's terse request—"See that the homework is done"—no doubt, parents all around the country responded defensively, with thoughts such as "That's easy for *you* to say. You don't have to deal with *my* kid." President Clinton didn't tell parents *how* to get the homework done. Are parents supposed to be homework inspectors? And what if parents see that the homework *isn't* done? Some respond by nagging, threatening, berating, and/or punishing their child. Others take the exact opposite approach: they do the homework with or even *for* their child. Still others consider it the teacher's responsibility to see that homework is completed. Most parents care deeply about their children's education and want to do the right thing. They wonder: How much help and what kind really proves helpful in the long run? And what kind of "help" is actually harmful? We'll answer these questions in this chapter and throughout the book.

True, homework blues would vanish if teachers simply stopped assigning homework. Some parents wish they would. Parents of youngsters in lower elementary grades often say that, after six hours cooped up in a classroom, children should be free to run and play. But homework has become a tradition for many good reasons. For one thing, mastery and retention are directly related to "time on task." Children need to practice and overlearn so that valuable skills stay with them. Teachers give homework assignments not only for practice but also to individualize academic experiences. Homework can be assigned to meet the varied needs of students, whether for extra math, spelling, or geography. Projects allow for further individualization and enrichment by helping children to develop research skills and use their creativity as they pursue special interests. Beyond helping students to acquire skills and knowledge, homework has other benefits. Doing homework all by themselves, children learn to enjoy the company of their own minds and the minds of those who visit them via the printed word. In addition, doing homework fosters independence, responsibility, and a sense of accomplishment.

But, as every parent of a school-age child knows, homework can also cause troubles. Some homework hassles are occasional and short-lived, not real problems, just now-and-then stressful situations. Others, *real* homework problems, reflect a pattern of destructive behavior, such as avoidance, dependence, or compulsive homework overkill. While the majority of homework difficulties originate with the student, some are created by well-meaning parents and teachers. Let's look at all three sides of this homework triangle.

Children and Homework

Children's homework difficulties can be grouped into two major categories: the first, we'll call homework obstacles or hurdles; the second are genuine homework problems. Homework hurdles are academic obstacles. A hurdle may develop when a child is absent from school for a few weeks because of illness, is confused by a new skill, has trouble organizing schoolwork, has a learning disability, or is a slow learner.

Academic hurdles can be cleared when parents and students are honest with the teacher about difficulties. Together, they can keep a hurdle from becoming a wall. Of course, there are many reasons why parents and children may not want to admit having academic difficulties. Their reluctance is understandable, but it doesn't negate the need for speaking out. A homework hurdle can become a homework problem if parents and teachers do not meet the student's needs with understanding, patience, encouragement, and realistic expectations. The child's capabilities (at that particular point in time) must be correctly assessed; then assignments and goals must be adjusted accordingly.

Unlike academic hurdles, homework problems are psychological or interpersonal problems, mostly involving family relationships, which affect the way children deal with homework. Sometimes a child unconsciously uses homework to accomplish an interpersonal goal, such as getting attention or getting revenge. Sometimes a psychological problem (for instance, fear of failure or an obsessive-compulsive disorder) results in an inability to handle homework successfully and without anguish. Dealing with these problems may require altering the family dynamics that have inspired the negative behavior. Let's look at a few examples:

Craig finishes his homework and does it carefully only when his mother is seated beside him, assuring him that each answer is correct or helping him if an answer is wrong.

Craig has a problem, and his parents are helping to perpetuate it. Perhaps he's using homework assignments as a way to get attention. Perhaps he's a perfectionist who must have everything just right. Perhaps he's not listening in class because he knows his mother will patiently reteach everything to him. Whatever the reason, his mother should gradually encourage more indepen-

THE FAMILY CIRCUS.   By Bil Keane

2-27
© 1995 Bil Keane, Inc.
Dist. by Cowles Synd., Inc.

"You misunderstand. I'm a
homework consultant, not a
homework subcontractor."

dence. She can check the first few problems and then let Craig handle the rest on his own. After all, most homework is assigned to provide practice. Practice is supposed to *make* perfect not *be* perfect. Without rejecting the child, Craig's mother should reject the role of nightly proofreader and tutor and help Craig to develop confidence in his own ability to do and check his work. The message should be loud and clear: homework is the *student's* responsibility.

Lindsay is usually up very late doing homework. She often expresses concern (sometimes accompanied by tears) about whether or not she'll finish her work on time and get a good grade.

Homework should not regularly produce so much anxiety that it makes a child unhappy. Lindsay and her parents should work out an after-school schedule together, one that gets her started on her homework earlier. But the bigger questions are: Why is Lindsay a chronic worrier? What is causing her intense anxiety? Lindsay's parents should ask themselves if they are sending her a silent message that they expect her to get top grades and will be disappointed with anything else. Is she competing with siblings and feeling that she can't keep pace? Children need to know that they are loved for who they *are*, not what they achieve. When there is too much anxiety attached to being a student, there's a higher risk of burnout. Chronic anxiety about homework is a problem that shouldn't be ignored. All "A's" does *not* mean that there's no homework problem.

Benita often forgets about her homework or forgets to bring home the books she needs in order to do it.

Chronic forgetting usually signifies a homework problem. Perhaps Benita is just immature and easily distracted. Perhaps her forgetfulness is a silent protest against something that's making her unhappy at home or at school. Then again, she may have discovered that not doing her homework earns her extra attention from her teacher and/or parents. (Children learn from infancy on that the squeaky wheel gets the oil.) It may be possible for the parents and the teacher, working together, to guide Benita toward more responsible behavior without pursuing the psychological reasons for her irresponsible behavior. An assignment notebook and a system of rewards for academic effort may do the trick.

Jason's parents are worried about their son's character because, when asked if he has homework, he lies and says, "No."

There is certainly a problem here, but what is it? It is probably *not* the fact that the child lies. The important question is this: Why has Jason been avoiding homework? Parents shouldn't assume that the cause is mere laziness or the lure of TV. There may be a more significant reason. Perhaps Jason didn't understand the work. He may have chosen to turn in no work rather than incorrect work. Most youngsters would rather appear uncooperative, defiant, even lazy, than take the chance of being labelled stupid. Of course, there are other possible explanations for Jason's behavior, which a three-way meeting—parents, teacher, and student—could uncover. Children lie for the same reasons adults do—to cover up their mistakes and keep out of trouble. Jason's parents should find out *why* their son is trapped in a corner from which the only escape seems to be a lie. When trying to alter a child's behavior, it's important to focus on one thing at a time. In this case, the first problem to deal with is the academic and/or emotional one. If frequent lying persists after the homework problem is solved, it can be dealt with then. Chances are that Jason's lying will stop when he no longer needs it as a protective mechanism.

As these examples reveal, an authentic homework problem is not an occasional event but a *pattern*. All children experience occasional brief periods of depression, stress, fatigue, and preoccupation that may cause them to forget their homework or to do a sloppy, incomplete job of it. However, a genuine homework problem is one that persists not just for a few days but for at least a few weeks.

Initially, it can be difficult for parents to distinguish between a homework hurdle and a homework problem. A parent-teacher conference can help by focusing on the following questions:

- Is the level of difficulty appropriate?
- Is there help when the child needs it?
- Is there proper affirmation when the child completes work acceptably?
- Are some assignments individualized to make them more interesting, challenging, creative, and relevant to each child's academic needs?

When the child has been given all these boosts and still does not clear the homework hurdle, parents and teachers must look further for causes and solutions. Suppose, for example, that a child has been involved in a conference with his parents and teacher and has agreed to a specific strategy designed to help him to get his homework in on time. If the student then continues to turn it in late, this unfulfilled promise or foot dragging indicates an emotional ingredient to his behavior.

It's important to realize that a particular child's problem may have both academic and emotional components. The child with academic weaknesses may develop emotional problems, such as homework anxiety and anger. The child with emotional problems may not pay attention in school and may, therefore, fall behind academically. (Chapter 5 covers emotional and interpersonal homework problems in greater detail.)

Many parents and teachers, working together, have had great success solving school-related problems with behavior modification techniques. These may range from a simple "thumbs up" gesture given by the teacher to a tangible reward for improved behavior given by the parent. (See Chapter 4 for specifics about homework contracts and other informal parent-child agreements.) If these incentives don't work, individual or family counseling is the next logical step.

Parents and Homework

Parents constitute the second side of the homework triangle. Many parents see education as *the* avenue to success in life, and they consider homework an integral part of their children's education. Homework is, after all, the main instrument that brings the child's school life into the home. It is through homework that parents find an opportunity to become acquainted and involved with their children's school life. This opportunity may lead parents with the best of intentions to make some significant mistakes. Let's take a look at some typical situations.

Some parents find it hard to let go and allow their children to take greater control over their own lives. Consider Charlie, for example. He leans over his son Jon's shoulder as his son composes essays on the computer. Charlie wants to help his son, so he makes suggestions and corrections as Jon writes. Does Jon have a homework problem? You bet he does—a problem named Charlie. Yes, parents should be involved in their children's education but not in ways that undermine their child's self-confidence and interfere with the youngster's natural desire to make his homework his own accomplishment. One of the greatest gifts that parents can give their children is the opportunity to handle their own responsibilities.

Other parents see their children as extensions of themselves. Their own self-esteem is tied to their children's successes and failures. Parents with this attitude may expect their children to duplicate their accomplishments or even exceed them. They may also force their children to comply with work habits and goals that worked well in their own school lives. Allison's parents are a case in point. They concentrate best in a silent environment. Allison, however, likes to do her homework while listening to music. Although her work is usually correct, her parents keep telling her that she can't possibly concentrate with "all that racket" going on. How do they know? Some children function well with background commotion. In fact, research has shown that listening to Mozart can enhance academic performance. Perhaps, for some young scholars, popular music might, too. If Allison is doing fine in school, there's nothing wrong with letting her decide if and when fast music slows her down.

Many parents despair because their children don't have the academic ambition to shoot for the moon. Well-educated parents of smart children often fall into this category. Malcolm's parents are a good example. They don't see Malcolm studying much at home. Their son's school grades are mostly Bs, high enough to satisfy Malcolm but not his parents. They believe that he's smart enough to be a B+ or A- student, and they want him to do his best. Is it their responsibility to turn their son into a top student? *Emphatically not.* Parents should see that their children learn the important skills and information taught in each grade. Beyond that, the child must decide whether he wants to work hard enough to be an outstanding student. Parents should not—indeed, cannot—regulate a child's academic enthusiasm and ambition. Nor should parents despair because they can't. In later academic years, the student who just coasted through elementary school (and even high school) may find a field of study that turns him on and suddenly develop the intellectual passion that his parents yearned for him to have at age nine.

Still other parents—Daphne's and Elsa's, for example— see problems where there are none. When Daphne sits down to do her homework, she spends some of the time just staring off into space. Her mother urges her to get right to work. But this ultra-pragmatic outlook, this obsession with using every moment to produce something tangible, is a lot less healthy than Daphne's daydreaming. Everyone daydreams—or should. It is a healthy, creative, replenishing activity. Perhaps daydreaming helps Daphne to produce more creative homework. Perhaps it supplies a needed break in the over-controlled, over-structured life of a typical American child. In either case Daphne's mother should not be trying to practice mind-control. Freedom of thought is a basic human right.

Elsa is on the phone most evenings, checking her math and social science answers with her best friend. Her parents want her to do her work alone. They don't realize that collaborative learning is "in," and for good reason. Students of all ages can learn much from one another. As long as Elsa is doing the work, not depending upon her friend to do it for her, there's probably nothing wrong with those nightly phone calls—except for their adverse effect upon the phone bill.

These examples illustrate that it's possible for parents to be too involved in their children's academic lives. Parents sometimes identify too closely with their children and impose their own habits, attitudes, and ambitions upon them. Children need parents who are interested in what they are doing in school and who ask about it. They need parents who are willing to help them with special projects when they need and want help. They need help that is given without anger or anxiety, help that doesn't confuse them, information that is correct, guidance that makes the task easier rather than more difficult, and assistance that leads them toward greater independence and self-confidence. Kids benefit immensely from parents who enrich their lives by exposing them to museums, music, sports, travel, and religion. But children also need the freedom to become themselves. Parents must step back and give their children the psychological space to do this.

Teachers and Homework

Teachers, too, can make mistakes regarding homework. Inexperienced teachers may assign too much or too little. Some teachers may not make the specifics of an assignment clear to students or may forget to individualize assignments to fit the various academic levels in a typical classroom. A parent should, without hostility, discuss troublesome homework assignments with the teacher. Teachers need feedback. They can't know how their students are reacting to their assignments if no one tells them.

Ross, a fifth-grade student, often spends three hours a night on homework. His parents are angry at the teacher for assigning so much work that Ross has no time to relax. Maybe the teacher is assigning too much. But another possibility is that Ross is delving into the topics more deeply than the teacher intended; or perhaps his academic skills are below the class average so assignments take him longer than the teacher realizes. However, Ross neither evades nor obsesses about his homework; instead, he plugs away at it. That's a healthy attitude. Still, he might get more rest if his parents let his teacher know about his homework struggles. (Chapter 8 provides advice about how to make tactful suggestions to your child's teacher.)

Mitchell says he doesn't need to do his homework because it's just more of what he already did correctly at school. His parents agree that he has already mastered the skills involved in most of his homework. Still, they can't condone his ignoring the assignments. Mitch's parents should explain two things to their son: (1) sometimes teachers want children to practice what they already know in order to increase speed and/or improve retention by "overlearning" the material; and (2) teachers don't have time to individualize every homework assignment to make it a precise fit with each child's level of expertise. When a particular assignment is easy for him, Mitch can do it quickly, so what's the point of refusing to do it? To keep his mind occupied, perhaps he can think of a creative way of doing the task. Another suggestion: Mitch might ask the teacher if he could (after demonstrating his mastery of the work assigned) tackle some more advanced work in its place. Some teachers will respond affirmatively and even enthusiastically to such a suggestion. But, if not, the bottom line is this: a successful and less stressful academic future is possible when a child accepts the teacher's authority instead of fighting it.

Whatever is causing difficulties with homework, honest discussion among all members of the homework triangle—parent, child, and teacher—goes a long way in the right direction, toward a better understanding of what's wrong and how it can be fixed.

2

Debunking Homework Myths

Few people take courses in parenting before tackling this perilous job. Learning to parent is more a matter of on-the-job training, based upon trial and error and the advice of predecessors. But as parenting tips are passed down from one generation to another, so are many harmful myths about childrearing. These myths affect the ways in which parents deal with homework hassles as well as other parenting issues. Discarding these misguided beliefs is one of the kindest acts that parents can do for themselves and their children.

Myth 1: Homework problems are about homework.

As we pointed out in Chapter 1, true homework problems are not about homework at all. Rather, they are symptoms of psychological or interpersonal family problems. One child regularly "forgets" to do homework or doesn't complete it. Another child routinely "remembers"—at 10:30 P.M. or later—that he or she absolutely *must* have some supplies for class the next morning. Another routinely sits doodling at his desk for hours but doesn't get his compositions written because no topic comes to mind. These students may be using homework assignments to accomplish something else—to express hostility, to get attention, or for some other emotional reason.

Likewise, parents who work on homework "with" their children, who see to it that no answer is ever incorrect, who protect their children from any disapproval at school, are playing out their own agendas. Perhaps they are having trouble untying the apron strings; perhaps they have a need for their children to be the best or a fear that their children cannot do even adequate work without their help. Counseling can help parents and children cope with the emotions underlying their homework hassles.

In some households parents argue about who should help the child with homework and how much help the child should be given. These kinds of arguments create anxiety for children. Parents need to reach an agreement about homework help outside the presence of the child and then present a united front.

Working on homework together can be a pleasant experience for both parent and child if the tutoring session is really about schoolwork and not about the parent and child trying to control each other. (More about control issues in Chapter 5.)

Myth 2: Good parents help their children with homework.

In recent years many educators and political leaders have accused American parents of abdicating their parenting responsibilities, especially when it comes to requiring their children to do homework in a timely and attentive fashion. In response, many parents have gone too far in the opposite direction, in the direction of too much parental intervention.

In a recent *Chicago Tribune* article, humorist Robert Hughes writes that having children in elementary school has eliminated difficult decisions about what to do with leisure time. "These days," Hughes writes, "my wife and I can relax in the knowledge that every evening for the foreseeable future will be spent doing homework." We hope not. Parents may provide occasional help in small doses when children are struggling with a new concept. But children who pay attention in school should be able to handle their homework independently most of the time, and that is clearly the goal. The chief obligation of parents in regard to homework is to be firm about their expectation that the homework be completed on time and be done adequately.

Of course, there are many other important roles for parents in the education of their children. Parents can teach their children strategies for memorizing and organizing. They can help their kids select topics for essays and projects. They can take them to the library (or to the computer) and demonstrate research techniques. They can contribute to their children's education via trips, family outings, family hobbies, and dinner-table discussions. Most of all, they can encourage effort and praise real accomplishment.

Myth 3: Every evening, parents should ask their children, "Do you have any homework?"

Why bother asking? The responsible student will do the work on time without being nagged and will resent the parents' questions because they imply a lack of trust. These questions are equally pointless when directed to the irresponsible student, who may not give honest answers. The student who has a history of homework-completion problems should have an assignment notebook that parents check daily. The responsible student can be asked about the *nature* of his or her homework, not just if there is any.

Myth 4: A parent should check a child's completed homework to be sure it's correct.

Long term, this pattern can be destructive. Homework is the student's responsibility. That includes deciding whether the math problems are done correctly and whether the essay is long enough and polished sufficiently to satisfy the teacher. If a child is not weaned from parental dependency, it can go on and on into adulthood. We know a father who drove four hours to his son's college town almost every weekend to tutor the young man in his engineering courses. We also know a mother who flew eight hundred miles to help her daughter (a graduate student) finish the paper she was about to pre-sent at a convention. Most parents want their adult children to be more self-sufficient and confident. Parents should get them moving in that direction beginning in elementary school.

We agree that there are times when it's a good idea to check a child's homework. If a first- or second-grader wants to show off his good work and receive some well-deserved praise, it's fine for parents to respond. When a child of any age is starting on some new skill and isn't sure if he or she is doing the homework correctly, the parent should certainly check the work if asked to do so. (But in this case it makes more sense to step in early after the child has done just a small part of the task. Why wait until the entire assignment is done incorrectly?) A third situation that calls for parental checking of homework is when the teacher recommends it.

When parents comment upon a child's math, they need to think of the glass as half full, not half empty. The negative parent shrieks, "You've gotten ten of these twenty problems wrong! Why are you so careless?" The affirmative parent says, "You got half of them right. I think you understand the process. See if you can find your errors in the ones I've circled."

In commenting upon a student's writing, parents must be care-ful not to apply adult standards to the work of a ten-year-old child. What looks like a terrible essay to an adult may actually be pretty good for a child of that age. It's also important to find something good to say about a child's piece of writing. There is usually at least one good idea or one well-expressed sentence even in a terrible essay.

Parental checking of homework may be necessary if the child has a homework completion problem (the work is often carelessly done, incomplete, etc.). But parental supervision should not go on forever. As soon as possible, the student should take over responsibility for evaluating his or her schoolwork.

Myth 5: Children must always do their schoolwork to the best of their ability.

Do adults do all their work to the best of their ability? Of course not. We all pace ourselves. We work harder and concentrate more when tackling tasks that are most important. Children should be allowed to do this also. Don't encourage compulsive perfectionism. Most children know which assignments are more important and which are less important. Parents shouldn't increase a child's anxiety about school by requiring him or her to please two bosses: parent and teacher.

Myth 6: Most children who have problems with homework are slow learners.

Not true. Kids across the academic spectrum turn in messy, incorrect work. Bright children, like most other children, do not always follow directions carefully. Nearly all children need help in developing good work habits, whether their intelligence quotient (IQ) is 90 or 190. So don't be horrified if your smart child makes a lot of dumb mistakes. Who doesn't? Scolding a child for making a lot of careless mistakes probably won't help; making a game of hunting for errors probably will.

Myth 7: Shutting off the TV is the answer to homework problems.

TV is not the enemy of homework, and parents who attack it as such are tilting at windmills. Children who regularly procrastinate or totally avoid homework usually do so because of fear, anger, or some other emotional problem. These are the enemies that must be defeated.

Forbidding TV to a child who is already unhappy for other reasons is cruel. Moreover, no TV at all leaves today's children in a cultural vacuum when conversing with their contemporaries. Also, many TV shows are wonderful educators. On the other hand, limiting TV viewing time and forbidding the viewing of violent shows are good ideas. And President Clinton was right when he suggested that TV and homework don't mix.

A household rule that all homework must be completed before children can watch TV might be necessary for the perennial homework procrastinator, but it's unnecessary for the diligent student who

wants to watch her favorite show before dinner and do her homework later.

Myth 8: Children are more likely to do their homework when they like their teacher.

Some parents are quick to make excuses for their children: "Johnny
doesn't do the homework for Mrs. G. because she's mean and he
hates her." In general, parents should not blame homework completion problems on the teacher. Children who don't have a conscious
or unconscious motive for *not* doing the homework will do it whether
they like the teacher or not. However, admittedly, if they like the
teacher, they may be more attentive in school and work harder on
assignments.

Myth 9: Parents shouldn't "bribe" kids to do their homework.

A bribe should not be confused with a reward. The word *bribe* has
negative denotations and connotations. It is something of value
offered in order to *corrupt* an individual, to convince the person to
do something illegal or immoral. A reward, on the other hand, is
given after the deed is done, and the behavior requested is generally
considered socially and/or morally positive.

When children have homework problems, rewards may be necessary to motivate a change in behavior. Some parents worry that if
they offer a reward for doing schoolwork this year, they will have to
continue doing so forever. But this is not the case. Eventually, the
rewards for keeping up with schoolwork come from the classroom.
Students are more comfortable in school when the teacher approves
of their behavior. There may also be an improvement in relationships
with classmates when students are no longer uncooperative non-
conformists. Finally, there is personal satisfaction and sometimes
even excitement in keeping up academically and understanding what
is being taught in school. Once children begin to put some effort into
their schoolwork, they see that doing it makes them happier, and

they are generally not motivated to return to their former unproductive behavior. (For more about rewards, see Chapter 4, "Drafting Homework Contracts.")

Myth 10: School is to a child's life what a job is to an adult's life.

Some parents try to motivate their children by saying something like this: "I go to work every day and work hard at my job. You should go to school every day and work hard at your job." There are shoe trees and pear trees, but they are quite different. So, too, is the academic work of a child extremely different from the work of an adult. When adults go to work, they sell their talents, skills, or products in order to make a living. When children go to school, they are involved not in an economic experience but in a developmental experience. True, the child's teacher can be compared to the working parent's boss, but, when pushed further, the school-job analogy doesn't hold up well. The child knows that parents choose a particular line of work (something they're good at and enjoy) and have the freedom to change jobs or change careers. The elementary school student, on the other hand, has virtually no options. The school, teacher, subjects, assignments, and classmates are all chosen by adults.

Rather than being compared to adult employment, academic work is more logically compared to play. (In Greek, the word for *education* is the same as the word for *play*.) Children's fantasy "play" deals with life's most serious issues, such as loss, pain, suffering, domination, dependence, and hatred. Their schooling, too, is a serious developmental experience that prepares them for adult participation in a complex world.

Myth 11: Parents are not responsible for the misconduct of their children.

Society seems to go through cycles on this point. Today, Americans are moving toward holding parents more accountable for their children's behavior. Some communities even have laws giving courts the right to fine parents whose teenagers are out past curfew or lock up parents whose kids are chronically truant.

Nearly all children make mistakes, test limits, and at times behave badly. When these incidents happen, some parents turn the other way, convincing themselves that "boys will be boys" or "she'll outgrow it." However, it's important to respond promptly and vigorously to a child's behavioral lapses, to provide clear guidelines regarding acceptable behavior and negative consequences for inappropriate behavior.

A family is a small community, the first and most important community that a child belongs to. A child who behaves badly in school embarrasses (perhaps even humiliates) his parents as well as any siblings attending that same school. Children know this is true, and, in many cases, that is precisely why they behave badly.

However, parents whose egos are damaged every time their children get a poor grade on a test are identifying far too closely with the children's daily lives and creating unnecessary stress. Every time these children slide academically, they must deal with their parents' disappointment as well as their own. It's an unfair burden.

Myth 12: Parents have an obligation to see that their children are happy.

No one can make anyone else happy. Parents of school-age children quickly discover that, as much as they want to make their children happy, they cannot control whether or not their children win the school spelling bee, make the basketball team, or get teased on the playground. Parents must set their sights a bit lower than bliss. What they need to do is protect their youngsters from danger, moderate their misery, guide them away from the conduct that is the source of their unhappiness, and help them develop the resources to make responsible decisions.

How does all this relate to homework? In a futile effort to protect their children from unhappy moments in school, parents often create dependency that will cause more unhappiness later. Consider this mother: Margie doesn't think that her second-grader, Alex, can be trusted to get his homework assignments written down correctly. In fact, sometimes he does get them wrong. When his mother suspects an error, she calls a parent of another child in the class to see exactly what the assignment was. Thus, she protects Alex from being scolded or getting a bad grade. She is making a big mistake. Unhappiness (in small doses) can be a good teacher. Alex will force himself to pay attention only after he suffers the consequences of not doing so.

Still, ask parents what they want most in the whole world, and they'll usually say for their youngsters to be happy. Happiness is a futile goal. However, it is a common by-product of a life filled with meaningful occupation and close, stable personal relationships. Raise children who are able to dedicate themselves to work they love and to people they love, and they'll stand a good chance of finding happiness on their own. And that's no myth.

3

Learning About Learning

For better or worse, parents are the most influential teachers their children will ever have. Parents teach their children in many ways—by providing examples, experiences, and values; by introducing kids to skills; and, when necessary, by helping with academics.

Most parental instruction is transmitted unconsciously. As family members share the years together, children are exposed to and learn ethical beliefs, religious customs, baseball rules, card games, VCR instructions, and so on. The knowledge goes from parent to child painlessly, via conversation and hands-on experience. When a mother shows her baby how to hold a spoon or a telephone, instruction is given patiently, repeatedly, and cheerfully until the child masters the skill. Rarely is there parental anguish because Johnny Next Door mastered the skill more quickly. When a father helps his daughter learn to balance her two-wheel bike and she heads down the path on her own, both teacher and learner feel triumphant, whether the learning process took two days or two months.

But when academics enter the picture, everything changes. Who's in the top reading group? Who got all As? Who won the spelling bee? Who's in the gifted program? Who needs tutoring? The teacher knows, the other children in the class know, and eventually the parents find out which kids are "smart" and which are not. Parents who were thrilled by their children's steady development in the early years may suddenly feel disappointed, even alarmed, when their children are not near the top of the academic heap.

When a child falls behind in school, what do parents do to compensate? There are two dangerous extremes. At one end of the spectrum is the parent that turns the child's evenings into a review of the school day. Drill, drill, drill until the child resents school, resents the parents, and develops a resounding hatred of academics. At the opposite end of the spectrum is the parent who concludes that his slow reader is destined for academic failure. Between these two extremes, there is also a lot of room for psychological injury. Parents most often enter a child's school life via the homework route. Hassles over homework can cause damage in at least two ways: by reducing a child's sense of competence and by hurting the parent-child relationship. Parents know but sometimes forget that children develop at different rates and have different learning styles. Last year's weak reader may catch on and catch up this year, especially with appropriate help and encouragement.

Even students making satisfactory academic progress can be victims of parental complaints. So long as there is a gap between what the parents want the child to achieve in school and the actual level of work the child is producing, there is fertile ground for trouble. Parents want to be effective facilitators of their children's academic learning. Understanding some facts and theories about the process of learning can help.

What Do We Know About Learning?

Even an average student has truly amazing mental capacities. "The human brain is the best organized, most functional three pounds of matter in the known universe," Professor Robert Sylwester points out in his well-known book *A Celebration of Neurons: An Educator's Guide to the Human Brain.* The brain possesses tens of billions of nerve cells (called neurons) and a much greater number of smaller cells that nourish and protect the neurons. Neurons are very small—about 30,000 could fit on a pinhead. Each neuron is capable of connecting to thousands of others, and through these connections information is sent and received. Information travels between parts of the brain and between the brain and spinal cord via chemical and electrical interactions. By adulthood, the average brain has made more than 100 trillion connections. That's a lot of brain power! With this capacity the human being can tend to many things at once—voluntary, conscious behavior (such as walking, talking, and eating), involuntary behavior (such as breathing), the emotions, and thought. The brain receives information from all parts of the body, which it uses to send directions to other parts of the body ("Get your finger off the hot pot handle!") or to store for later use.

All children have an innate desire to learn. It seems to parents that children ask a million questions a minute. Why? They want to make sense of the world. Their minds are searching for challenges, for information that will enable them to build upon what they already know. In his book *Learning Makes Sense*, John Abbott, the director of London's Education 2000 Foundation, makes the following point: "Learning is a most natural activity—as fundamental and instinctive as the sex drive." Renate and Geoffrey Caine, leading synthesizers of current brain research, put it this way in *Making Connections: Teaching and the Human Brain*: "The search for meaning (making sense of our experiences) is survival-oriented and basic to the human brain." What should this realization suggest to parents? If a child is uninterested in learning, something is wrong, and the parents should work with the school to find out what it is.

Parents matter. How good a student will Brian be? That depends upon a number of factors, many of which can be influenced by his parents. It is likely that the main circuitry of the brain is genetically determined, and yes, the quality of the mind Brian inherits will affect his learning capabilities.

Researchers have found that identical twins raised apart still have remarkably similar interests, personalities, and IQ scores. But the importance of innate "brain power" is often overestimated. In a comprehensive study reported in the journal *Nature* (August 1997), researchers did a statistical analysis of 212 earlier studies and concluded that genes account for only 48 percent of the factors that determine IQ. Environment, including prenatal conditions, accounts for the rest. This study suggests that inadequate prenatal care may be one reason why poorer people generally score lower on IQ tests.

The question of which dominates—nature (inherited traits) or nurture (experiences)—is, says Robert Sylwester, "like trying to determine which hand contributed most to the sound of hands clapping." Clearly, the mental capacity of a given child is affected by both. Appropriate childhood experiences are extremely important in brain development, and parental attitudes greatly influence a child's responses to the academic environment.

Why are parents so important? Compared to other animals, the human infant is extremely dependent and vulnerable for a very long period of time. Other animals, born with instincts in a much more complete state, can more quickly learn to feed themselves, take care of themselves, be "on their own." The human animal develops its instincts much more slowly, through its relationships to primary caregivers. As a result, there are strong social and emotional components to human learning.

School-age children sometimes act as if no one outside their peer group matters to them, but in reality they care very much about what parents, teachers, and other important adults in their lives think of them. Their learning is affected, positively or negatively, by the attitudes of the adults who are raising them. But it is not enough to tell children that education is important and knowledge exciting. What happens at home must demonstrate that truth.

The brain is altered by experience. The more the brain is used, the more connections grow. Scientists call this characteristic *brain plasticity*. "Use it or lose it"—something we often say to encourage people to exercise their muscles—is equally important in terms of using the mind. A transnational organization of scholars called The 21st Century Learning Initiatives describes it this way: "The human brain is a living, unique, ever-changing organism that grows and reshapes itself in response to challenge, with elements that wither through lack of use." This idea has vastly important implications for parents, who can supply appropriate experiences and intellectual challenges at various stages of their children's development.

Timing is important. Connections within the brain develop most rapidly during the first three years of life. Young children who have been deprived of all-important sensory experiences—the human voice, a loving touch, colorful possessions to play with, music—will have smaller brains and fewer connections between neurons than youngsters who have been stimulated by a rich array of sights, sounds, and tactile stimuli. When the deprivation is severe enough, children's brains resemble those of Alzheimer's patients. Researchers have found similar effects upon animals growing up in zoos. They tend to have smaller brains than animals living in the wild, a more stimulating environment. Brain wiring of neural connections reaches its peak at age three. During the next two years of their lives, children lose about 40 percent of the brain cells they were born with, in a normal process called *neural pruning*.

Throughout childhood, there are optimum periods, often referred to as *windows of opportunity*, when children's brains are best equipped to learn certain kinds of material. We know, for example, that children learn a second language most easily when they are preschoolers. According to some researchers, if the study of a second language is postponed until age eleven, the student will never speak the language like a native. Yet, many school systems do not begin second language instruction until students are in the upper elementary grades or even in high school. However, parents can opt to introduce second language studies much earlier. Many do so by speaking their native language to their children at home or by sending children to religious or ethnic institutions that teach a foreign language.

Researchers also tell us that early exposure to music (both listening and playing) develops the brain in ways that improve the child's ability to reason and to do mathematics. Again, parents can bring music into the young child's life for its own sake, for the joy it brings, and for the possible benefits to brain development.

What should all this information about early brain development mean to parents? There is a danger that some parents, in a frantic attempt to develop their children's minds to their maximum potential, will rush them from one activity to the next, wearing everyone out and making parenting more exhausting than it needs to be. Another danger is that parents and educators make errors in timing by trying to teach certain concepts too soon. Children must be developmentally ready to handle certain concepts or they just won't "get it." A three-year-old will be thrilled by (and benefit greatly from) a visit to a petting zoo, a sensory experience. But that same child will probably find a tour of Lincoln's home excruciatingly boring. The historical perspective just isn't there yet.

Learning is primarily a social, not a solitary, activity. Traditionally, most people have thought of studying as an activity carried out independently in a quiet room with books and papers. Of course, many mental activities—such as memorizing, reviewing, practicing, and brainstorming for creative ideas—can be successfully accomplished alone. But a great deal of learning occurs most effectively in an environment that is collaborative, that involves conversation, exchange of ideas, experimentation, and group problem solving. Learning also takes on an emotional impetus when it occurs in a social setting. When children choose to study together (in person, on the phone, or via E-mail), they are not wasting time. They are giving their studying a social context it may need to be meaningful, or at least bearable, as in the case of memorizing the multiplication tables and other such tedious chores.

Children learn best by doing. John Dewey, noted twentieth-century American philosopher and educational theorist, emphasized this idea. And we find a similar thought in this Chinese proverb: "Tell me, and I'll forget; show me, and I may remember; involve me, and I'll understand." Learning and doing are the Siamese twins of education. The most effective learning is embedded in experience. When what we've taught students changes their *behavior*, then we know it has truly been learned.

Learning involves much more than just rational thought. We educate our bodies as well as our minds, and, indeed, all learning is a physiological as well as a mental process. Emotions are an important part of learning too. Students understand better and remember longer when they are emotionally engaged in what they are studying.

Today's students must prepare to be life-long learners. Technology is changing the world so rapidly that we know today's students will have to keep learning forever and perhaps even change careers several times during their adult lives. The home and the school must share responsibility for teaching children to take greater responsibility for their own learning.

What Is Intelligence?

"Is my child smart?" Nearly every parent wonders about this and hopes the answer is "Yes." But just what does this label of intelligence actually mean? For many years intelligence was considered a single quality that human beings possessed to a greater or lesser degree. Today the prevailing view is quite different. Scholars have discovered that different kinds of information are processed in different areas of the brain. Thus, it is easy to understand that a person's mental capacities vary from one field of study to another.

With the 1983 publication of psychologist Howard Gardner's influential book *Frames of Mind: The Theory of Multiple Intelligences*, the word *intelligence* developed a plural form. Gardner defines an intelligence as "the ability to solve problems, or to create products, that are valued within one or more cultural settings." In other words, intelligence is related to what a person can do and share. Gardner's seven intelligences are described as follows:

- *linguistic intelligence*—the capacity to communicate (via gestures, speech, or writing), to persuade, retain information, explain, or discuss the nature of language itself

- *musical intelligence*—ability in listening, playing, and/or composing music
- *logical-mathematical intelligence*—the ability to do abstract
  thinking in these areas (not simply the ability to calculate
  rapidly)
- *spatial intelligence*—a primarily visual ability that allows a person to accurately see and interact with objects in the environment. (People with spatial intelligence include sculptors,
  inventors, skilled map readers, and pilots. A blind or blind-
  folded chess player also utilizes spatial intelligence.)
- *bodily-kinesthetic intelligence*—skill in the use of the human
  body (such as is possessed by an athlete or a dancer) or skill
  in manipulating objects (such as that displayed by the violin-
  ist or auto mechanic)
- *personal intelligences*—(1) *the sense of self*: in Gardner's words
  "access to one's own feeling life" and the ability to draw upon
  these feelings to understand and guide one's behavior. This
  intelligence is likely to be evident in the work of a poet, nov-
  elist, or psychologist. (2) *interpersonal intelligence*: the ability to
  understand, in Gardner's words, the "moods, temperaments,
  motivations, and intentions" of others. Teenagers with this
  kind of ability may get elected class president. Adults with
  interpersonal intelligence are likely to have successful relationships and satisfying careers that involve working closely
  with others.

By 1997 Gardner had expanded his well-known list of intelligences to include an eighth. It is identified (in *Extraordinary Minds*)
as "the apprehension of the natural world, as epitomized by skilled
hunters or botanists."

These innate intelligences are abilities that may or may not be
fully developed. They are more likely to be realized when appropriate experiences are provided (such as encouragement and instruction), when obstacles do not exist (such as parental disapproval or a
physical impairment), and when the person is eager to devote time
and energy to the activity. Thus, the little girl who dreams of becoming a figure-skating champion will get closer to her dream if her par-

ents are willing to pay for private lessons, if her falls don't lead to serious injuries, and, most important, if she's willing to practice several hours a day.

These eight intelligences do not operate in isolation. As Gardner explains, "Nearly all cultural roles exploit more than one intelligence." Consider, for example, the actor. The intelligences he utilizes are likely to include at least linguistic, bodily-kinesthetic, and interpersonal.

Gardner's theory of intelligences has much to say to parents. Clearly, this broader view of intelligence suggests that parents cannot discover how intelligent their child is simply by obtaining an intelligence quotient (IQ) score. IQ tests evaluate verbal and mathematical-logical abilities but not the other intelligences. An IQ score is *not* the sum total of a child's mental capacity or potential. It is *not* a measure of purely innate talent (as opposed to learned information); nor does it measure creativity, initiative, or motivation, all of which affect academic achievement. Still, many school systems use IQ scores for various purposes. They are usually part of the formula for selecting children for a gifted program. They are also sometimes indicators of problems—if a child with a high IQ is doing poor schoolwork, the discrepancy could be a sign of a learning disability or an emotional disturbance. An IQ score can be a valuable piece of the total picture of a child, but it should never be viewed as a measure of the child's total mental capacity.

Like Gardner, Daniel Goleman includes emotional and social factors in his definition of intelligence. To some people the title of his 1995 bestseller, *Emotional Intelligence*, might seem an oxymoron (like a "happy problem" or "cruel kindness"). After all, it is traditional to equate intelligence with rational thought and to consider emotional responses irrational. To others the title might be just downright confusing. Just what is emotional intelligence, and who has it? As Goleman explains it, emotionally intelligent people understand their own feelings and can control their impulses, especially negative ones. They can stop and think before acting upon anger or jealousy. Of course, emotional intelligence is not a single quality. It involves a whole series of strengths; people may possess many or few and to a greater or lesser degree. Some of these have to do with self-control—for example, having the discipline to keep working on a task even after it becomes frustrating or boring. Some kinds of emotional intelligence relate to getting along with others: empathy, compassion, leadership skills, or the ability to sense the unspoken feelings of companions.

Emotional intelligence has a great deal to do with academic success, Goleman points out: "A child's readiness for school depends on the most basic of all knowledge, *how* to learn." Goleman then lists the seven key ingredients of this capacity—confidence, curiosity, intentionality (the wish and capacity to have an impact, and to act upon that with persistence), self-control, relatedness (the ability to engage with others), the capacity to communicate, and cooperativeness.

Where do these abilities come from? To some extent they are innate. For example, a child may be timid because of certain inherited characteristics affecting brain chemistry. A tendency to be optimistic or pessimistic may also be genetic. But emotional intelligence can be taught, and inherited tendencies can be adjusted. Children can learn by example, discussion, and/or experience. Goleman points out a fact that should be reassuring to parents: "several brain areas critical for emotional life are among the slowest to mature. . . . The frontal lobes—seat of emotional self-control, understanding, and artful response—continue to develop into late adolescence, until somewhere between sixteen and eighteen years of age." There is ample time for parents to help their children develop the emotional capacities that will lead to greater contentment and achievement.

Finally, parents should help children develop these important elements in our operating definition of intelligence: good judgment, good problem-solving skills, and good old-fashioned common sense.

What About Memory?

"Much learning does not teach a man to have intelligence," said the Greek philosopher Heraclitus about 2,500 years ago. Today, most people still recognize this distinction between the possession of facts and the ability to use knowledge well in thought and action. Still, we cannot ignore the fact that memory is an important part of learning.

The student needs information with which to think, create, and judge.

The ability to store and recall information is what we commonly call *memory*. Without memory, learning would be impossible. When a student learns something new, chemical changes occur in the brain. New pathways, known as *memory traces*, develop between neurons, and these traces, when activated, create the thoughts called memories. There are two general types of memory: motor skill and factual. There are also three memory levels: immediate, short-term, and long-term. Immediate memory lasts just a few seconds—the time it takes to see Mary's red dress. Short-term memory is a matter of a minute or two—perhaps as long as it takes to dial the phone number the operator just gave you. Long-term memory may last a lifetime. (You'll never forget Aunt Edna's face.) But much academic knowledge that students expect to have and hold forever disappears if not used. One of the goals of education is to transfer information from short-term to long-term memory. As students discover, long-term retention is more likely when material is learned over a greater period of time and when practice (repetition) is involved in the learning. There are also strategies that can improve memory. (See Chapter 7.)

Why did Jennifer get a low grade on her history test? "I couldn't help it. I have a bad memory" goes the familiar explanation. Is that just an excuse, or do some children have poorer memories than others? What about the student who can't remember Spanish vocabulary words but has his lines for the school play down cold? And what about the spelling whiz who can't remember to bring his science book home? No doubt, children remember more easily whatever seems interesting or useful to them. But it is also possible that memory is not a single ability. There may be a different memory potential for each of Gardner's intelligences.

What Inhibits Learning?

Certainly one reason that children prefer a computer tutorial to a live tutor is that the computer is a nonjudgmental evaluator of its user. It tells children they're wrong but never that they're stupid. Moreover, the computer has infinite patience, allowing any number of second chances. When parents try to help their children learn, they should adopt some of the computer's virtues. Parents who want to help their children develop a love of learning should avoid creating associations between academic work and such negative feelings as anger, shame, jealousy, and feelings of inadequacy. Here are a few "don'ts" to make the point clear.

Don't make comparisons. Children should not be compared academically to their friends, cousins, parents, or siblings. If parents cannot resist making such comparisons, at least they should do so privately, when their children are not present. Even the child who is identified as the superior one doesn't benefit from being compared. Anita, told that her grades are much better than cousin Barbara's, knows that her mother is pleased. But now Anita must live with the anxiety that cousin Barbara may catch up or even surpass her next semester, and then Mother will be displeased. Anita's good work should be valued for its own sake, not because it surpasses a rival's.

Comparisons are even more devastating to the child with the lesser accomplishment. Some parents compare their kids to themselves: "When I was in fourth grade, I was a whiz at long division." Other parents compare siblings: "Look at how neat your sister's homework is. Why can't you do that?" Still other parents compare kids to other kids: "Stanley's mother told me that Stanley got all As on his last report card." Even when the parent doesn't complete the comparison aloud, the child gets the point: Stanley's mother is proud of him, but you're not proud of me. Making a child feel bad about what has already happened and can't be changed is not productive. It is also likely to make the child feel angry at the parent and hostile toward the "superior" child. Comparisons are an attempt to motivate by fueling the competitive spirit. But today most educators agree that cooperation and teamwork provide more nourishing food for thought.

Don't make generalizations. "You always . . ." or "You never . . ." statements make a child defensive. The focus should be on good patterns needed for the future rather than on unsuccessful behaviors that have led to failure in the past. Generalizations in the form of labels (such as "You're lazy. You don't try hard enough.") may backfire by giving the child an excuse for inappropriate behavior and encouraging her to live up to the label.

Don't stress mistakes. "Look at all these spelling errors. Why are you so careless?" When looking over a child's work, most parents immediately spot what's wrong. What's right is taken for granted; what's wrong is discussed with the child, sometimes in a deprecating tone. It's important for parents to notice and comment upon what Bobby did right: he remembered to bring home the book and the assignment; he sat down and did the work; and he completed all the problems. These are all positives that a child can be praised for. Whatever part of the assignment is done correctly is yet another positive. Even if the work is mostly wrong, the fact that Bobby tried to do it on his own is worthy of comment and compliment. Mistakes should be discussed in a calm, neutral fashion without the emotional overtones of Mom's anger, annoyance, or disappointment.

Mistakes should not be harped upon but neither should they be ignored. Some parents (and some teachers) are onto the self-esteem bandwagon. They fear that criticism will hurt Rachel's feelings and cause her to think less of herself. They worry about her poor schoolwork, but they worry silently. But their reasoning should be reversed. Helping children become more competent leads to greater freedom from excessive self-criticism. Children will be happier and more successful if they know they can do what is expected of them academically at the various grade levels.

Don't shame your child. Bad reports from teachers usually make parents angry, and they may find themselves screaming ineffective messages like these: "You should be ashamed of yourself!" "How could you do a terrible thing like that?" "Don't you have any sense at all?" And, finally, the all-encompassing "You're impossible!" These kinds of responses do not encourage better behavior; they only encourage self-hatred. The focus should be on ways to correct problems rather than on how bad the child should feel because something has gone wrong.

Don't use an emotional ploy. "You're driving me crazy," a desperate parent tells the kid who isn't performing well in school. This child is being urged to do well in school in order to improve the parent's mood. But it is not the child's obligation to make the parent happy. Besides, parental happiness is not the reason we want children to do well in school. The real reason for academic effort? The family values education and believes that the child who keeps growing intellectually will have a happier, more meaningful life. Even if we can't prove it, this is the message we must send if we expect children to take schoolwork and homework seriously.

Don't threaten. Threats make some children defiant, bringing about precisely the negative result that the threat was intended to avoid. And even if the threat makes the child want to comply, fear of punishment distracts a student from learning tasks. According to Renate and Geoffrey Caine, under perceived threat the brain "becomes less flexible and reverts to primitive attitudes and procedures." To maximize learning, they recommend "an atmosphere of relaxed alertness, involving low threat and high challenge."

Don't scare kids by expressing expectations of high accomplishment. Tiffany, a third grader, had been a slow reader. Tutoring helped, and she was making progress. Her mother, with the best of intentions, offered this "encouraging" comment: "Soon you'll be the best reader in the class." Tiffany's response? "I wish I was dead." Tiffany's mom needs to help her daughter recognize and gain confidence from the progress she's already made, not burden her with overwhelming expectations.

Don't scoff at homework assignments. "Memorize the capital cities of all fifty states? What a waste of time!" Parents may feel this way about some homework assignments, but it's a bad idea to say so. Children need to believe that what their teachers are asking them to learn is worth learning. Parents should not undermine a child's respect for the teacher and the schoolwork being assigned.

What Qualities Make a Good Student?

Whether we label them *intelligences* or not, good work habits and positive attitudes toward learning are as important as innate linguistic and logical capacities in the development of an academically successful student. The good news is that, if children don't develop these habits and attitudes on their own, they can be taught or at least encouraged.

First of all, academic success demands perseverance, persistence, time on task to gain a thorough understanding of new material, and willingness to practice new skills. The child who doesn't give up or get discouraged or distracted easily, who gives schoolwork and homework the attention it requires, is, of course, likely to do better.

In *Emotional Intelligence*, Goleman's oft-quoted marshmallow story describes a research project that links academic success and the ability to control impulses and postpone gratification. Four-year-olds were given a marshmallow and told that, if they could resist eating their treat until the researcher returned to the room, they would get a second marshmallow. When these same children were studied again as high school seniors, researchers found that those WHO HAD BEEN ABLE to resist the marshmallow had average Scholastic Aptitude Test (SAT) scores 210 points higher than those who gave in to the marshmallow temptation. (Those who had been able to defer gratification were also more academically and socially competent teenagers.)

Motivation is all-important. The child who considers schoolwork a serious responsibility and who wants to learn what the teacher is trying to convey will make satisfactory progress even with average ability. Homework contracts (parent-child agreements that offer rewards for academic effort) are a good way to stimulate motivation. (See Chapter 4 for details.)

The good student pays attention to what is assigned and plans ahead to be sure the work gets done. The child with good organizational skills estimates how many hours will be needed to complete the work, breaks assignments down into manageable segments, and schedules the most difficult tasks for times when his or her mind is most alert. Organizational skills such as these help a child avoid being swamped, anxious, and chronically behind.

Resourcefulness is another trait that leads to satisfactory academic progress. Polina is able to predict problems she might have with homework and to ask her teacher the right questions to avoid later difficulty and frustration. She is assertive. She doesn't leave school without understanding exactly what the assignment is and when it is due. If she needs help in doing the work, she takes charge of the situation to see that she gets it. The next time a similar assignment is given, Polina will be able to do it independently. Her behavior is not to be confused with that of Gail, a dependent child, who seeks help to get the assignment done but is not interested in becoming more self-sufficient.

Confidence is important too as Goleman pointed out. In a paper entitled "Self-Efficacy Beliefs in Academic Settings," Frank Pajares summarizes these research findings: Most children are overconfident about their academic abilities, and that turns out to be a good thing. While realistic appraisals of their abilities serve students well, it seems that slight overestimation is even better because it leads to increased effort and persistence. Less confident students are more reluctant to try new tasks and more likely to give up when they get tough. Girls, particularly at higher academic levels, tend toward underconfidence. Parents should be aware of this and try to help their daughters develop more realistic and affirmative evaluations of their abilities. Gifted girls, one study indicates, are especially susceptible to underconfidence.

Finally, the child who feels accepted, feels a sense of belonging, is likely to do better in school than the student who feels alienated and/or excluded from the social milieu of the classroom. Parents can help their children learn to become active, contributing members of their school group by being involved in school functions themselves. Parents who attend school meetings, come to school shows, volunteer to accompany student groups on trips, become active in the PTA, and/or serve as volunteer tutors are modeling participatory behavior. They are also showing their children that they value the school and the work it does. Moreover, parents who have regular contact with the school staff gain greater and more frequent insights into how their children are doing there.

The bottom line is that parents cannot simply send a child to school and assume that the school will educate the child. Parents must be *partners* (though not intruders) in the education of their children. Parents can help schools teach facts and skills. In addition, parents are the primary teachers of values regarding education. Therefore, they can impart to their children a love of learning and a desire to use knowledge in socially constructive ways.

4

Drafting the Homework Contract

What's a Contract?

In many households parents establish rules about studying: "No TV until your homework is done." "Mandatory study time—from 7 to 8:30 P.M." These rules may work well, providing the structure that children need, helping them to plan ahead and give their schoolwork the time and concentration required. However, these rules set up by parents are not contracts.

A *contract* is an agreement between consenting parties. To most people the word suggests a long, complicated written document spelling out, in excruciating detail, a legal agreement between adults. But contracts can also be made with kids as a way of shaping their behavior. Contracts with kids don't need to be in writing and should not be complicated. But they must be crystal clear and mutually binding. A contract can be suggested by any adult interested in helping a child develop some positive behavior or eliminate negative behavior. Moreover, simple contracts can be successful even with very young children. Here are some examples of nonacademic contracts. They were not ideal contracts, but, nevertheless, they worked.

Howard was four years old when he visited a children's dentist. First, the dentist tried to persuade his new patient that sucking his finger wasn't good for either his teeth or his finger. Howard's defensive response: "You're not a finger doctor." Then, the dentist tried a different approach. He made an offer the little boy just couldn't refuse: if Howard could stop sucking his finger for thirty days in a row, the dentist would give him a prize. Howard and his mother marked off the days on the calendar. When a month had gone by, Howard received his reward—a huge red truck. This contract might have failed because Howard, not knowing what his prize would be, might have been insufficiently motivated to carry out his part of the bargain. But then, most children try to be good before Christmas even though they don't know exactly how Santa will reward their virtue. Even a contract that's less than ideal can motivate improved behavior.

Arthur's mother was determined that her six-year-old son learn to swim. In truth, she was annoyed, disappointed, even angry that her son was afraid and unwilling to try. Belittling him for his fears or shaming him with reminders that all his friends could swim were not good options. Enter the contract. The mother asked her son what he would like for a prize when he learned how to swim the width of the pool. They agreed that the prize would be a particular computer game that Arthur wanted. Arthur's mother enrolled her son in swimming classes, and within a month he had traversed the pool and earned his reward. The contract accomplished its goal, even though it was not ideally structured. An even better contract would have rewarded effort—for example, given points toward his prize every time Arthur went to swim class and tried.

A good contract provides an incentive to do (or not do) something for a specific reward. It doesn't need to be signed in blood or even in ink. A verbal agreement is fine for kids, though some might take it more seriously if there is a written document. Contracts are a way of shaping behavior from what is less desirable to what is more desirable. They are examples of what social scientists call *behavior modification*. This technique does not deal with the causes of behavior, does not ask why the person is behaving inappropriately. It simply tries to alter (and improve) behavior by the manipulation of rewards and punishments. Contracts can be used to modify behavior of young children, teenagers, and even adults. Tom frequently annoyed and embarrassed his wife by joking with friends about her obesity. Following the advice of a marriage counselor, the husband and wife made a deal: every time Tom mentioned his wife's size in public, he would have to do the dinner dishes the next evening. To avoid dishpan hands, Tom quickly learned to hold his tongue.

This book is certainly not recommending behavior modification as the only technique to utilize in childrearing. Often, parents should try to figure out or find out why their child is behaving in a particular way in matters of homework completion as in other matters. But when academic causes of homework avoidance have been ruled out, when it is clear that the student is capable of doing the assignments, then the contract is a good approach to try.

Specifically, what is a homework contract? It is an agreement between a child and the parent(s) or the teacher. It provides an incentive for the child to make a consistent effort to engage in schoolwork. It does so by breaking down larger tasks or goals into small, manageable, clearly defined segments and by rewarding slight but noticeable changes promptly and predictably.

When is a contract needed? It should be considered when homework avoidance is a *pattern* and probably due to emotional causes. Almost every child has occasional bad homework days due to illness, family crises, moving, squabbles with friends, and so on. These short-term lapses in otherwise responsible behavior can better be handled with short-term emotional support than with longer-term incentives. Homework avoidance includes such behavior as "forgetting" to do assignments, turning in incomplete assignments, and procrastinating about getting to homework tasks. Possible causes of homework avoidance will be discussed in Chapter 5. But without delving into the reasons, a contract can encourage change.

Who should suggest a contract? The idea usually comes from the parent or the teacher. Many teachers make contracts with individual students without involving their parents at all. Melanie frequently interrupted her teacher when he was in the middle of an explanation to the class. To encourage her efforts to hold off on her questions, he offered this reward: a thumbs-up gesture if Melanie got through fifteen minutes without interrupting. Believe it or not, that simple reward was sufficient motivation to keep Melanie quiet. Why? Thumbs up told Melanie that her teacher noticed and appreciated her effort.

Some contracts are worked out at joint meetings with input from the teacher, parent(s), and child. Others are arranged at home, primarily between parent(s) and child, but perhaps also involving some brief daily or weekly response from the teacher indicating whether the child's part of the contract was fulfilled satisfactorily. In some cases the teacher is totally unaware of a homework problem because the homework is always completed and turned in promptly. However, to make this happen, the parents may be spending every evening at the child's beck and call. How can parents avoid being manipulated by children in this way? Contract to the rescue!

Why are homework contracts so successful? Consider this common family situation when there is no contract: a nightly power struggle ensues, with parents trying to get the child to do an adequate job of completing homework and the child resisting, trying to slide by with as little effort as possible. The creation of a contract turns the parent from the opponent into a teammate or at least an enthusiastic cheerleader. A contract encourages a child to plan ahead and schedule time for work. When there is a contract, both the child and the parents are under greater control, and their behavior is predictable. There are fewer arguments about when to study, how much to study, and how much parental help to expect.

Although it's not necessary to write down the contract, this certainly can be done. A simple form such as the one on page 45 will suffice in most cases.

Many contracts involve a system of points, checks, stars, etc., given on a daily basis and leading to a tangible reward when a stated number of marks has been earned. This method allows for small,

---

Homework Contract

Date: _____

_____ (student's name)

agrees to

_____

_____

_____ (parent or teacher's name)

agrees to

_____

_____

_____

---

immediate "payment" for completing various segments of homework tasks. If the student is a typical homework avoider, the contract may include four parts of the task: (1) writing the homework assignment(s) correctly in the assignment book; (2) remembering to bring home whatever is needed (textbook, teacher's handout, supplies, etc.) to do that evening's homework; (3) spending the agreed-upon amount of time working on homework; and (4) completing the task. A chart for recording daily points for accomplishing these tasks might look like the one shown on page 46.

It's useful to note which column has the highest score and which of the four tasks is giving the student the most trouble. Then parent and child can discuss why and come up with strategies to improve that specific score the following week.

Record of Homework Performance				

Week of:_____

	Assignment book filled in and taken home	Needed papers and textbooks brought home	Forty-minute study period completed	All homework completed on time
Monday				
Tuesday				
Wednesday				
Thursday				
Friday				
Saturday or Sunday				
Weekly point total: ____				

The child receives points each day for each task completed. There should be an agreed-upon weekly reward for earning 75 percent of the total possible number of points. More points can be given for more significant tasks such as spending the agreed-upon amount of time on homework and finishing the work. There can also be bonus points for a perfect day.

Of course, the tasks to be rewarded are those which have been areas of weakness. (Areas of strength are self-rewarding.) If the child brings home his school books but needs frequent reminders to open them up, then a series of contracts would reward the child for getting to work with a gradually declining number of reminders.

What Worries Parents About Contracts?

Suggesting contracts to parents often elicits one of these responses:

"We don't believe in bribes."

"Once we start offering a reward for doing homework, we'll have to continue doing so for Jeremy's entire school life."

"The other children in the family will also feel entitled to 'payment' for doing their schoolwork."

But none of these concerns is a real problem. First, a reward is not a bribe. A bribe is an incentive given to induce a person to do something wrong—something illegal or immoral or both. A bribe is offered by someone who will benefit from the action, and it compromises the character of the person accepting it. A reward for schoolwork completion, on the other hand, encourages a child to improve behavior, to do something that is in the child's best interest.

Second, contracts don't have to go on forever. To quote the great nineteenth-century American author Ralph Waldo Emerson, "The reward of a thing well done is to have done it." There are intrinsic rewards—feelings of personal satisfaction in accomplishment—that are the most meaningful form of "payment" for academic progress. There are also extrinsic rewards in terms of relationships. Students who are not doing their work must endure the disapproval of parents and teachers and the derision of classmates. When former slackers begin to accept their academic responsibilities, school and home life become more pleasant. Rarely are kids motivated to return to the shameful position of being nonproducing students.

When one child in the family has a homework contract, will siblings also demand one? Probably not. The intrinsic rewards of learning and the status that comes with being successful in school continue to be sufficient to motivate high-achieving students. It is extremely unlikely that a productive student will decide to stop doing schoolwork until offered some extrinsic reward. Children often demand that their parents be "fair." But they need to understand that in matters of schoolwork, what's fair is not equal assistance but whatever help meets each child's needs.

What Makes a Good Contract?

A contract *will* work—if it is a good contract. As you develop a homework contract, consider the following suggestions.

Keep it simple. Many children who don't complete their homework fall behind because of inattention and/or poor organizational skills. A long, complicated contract will overwhelm them, and they will not be able to respond successfully to its terms. Also, a contract that requires parents to put forth a lot of time and effort is likely to fail. Within a week parents are likely to get weary of the tedious routine, and the contract will go by the wayside. Keep it simple enough so that it doesn't become confusing to the child or a burden to the parent.

Begin at the child's baseline. Keep expectations reasonable. Eventually, you want your child to spend an hour a day on homework. Right now, he spends barely ten minutes. In the initial contract, put in a study time period of ten or fifteen minutes. Remember, the contract should be designed to shape behavior gradually. When you renegotiate the terms in the following weeks, gradually increase the study time requirement.

Negotiate the contract. The child should work with the parent in developing the terms of the contract. What can be negotiated? The amount of time spent studying, the degree of completeness required, and the reward—all of these must be discussed. A contract is an *agreement*. The child must agree to put forth so much effort for a particular reward. If the child feels that the work required is not being amply rewarded, the contract will fail. Both parties, parent and child, must feel that the contract is fair and reasonable.

Consult the teacher. It's a good idea to talk to the teacher about the homework contract. A three-way conference (child, teacher, and parent) can help to clarify the goals. The parent and the student need to get from the teacher a clear understanding of what the child needs to do. Then the parent and child can work out a series of agreements that gradually move the youngster toward those goals. However, parents and students must remember that the teacher has a roomful of students and cannot spend a lot of time responding to parental queries about the quality of each student's nightly homework. Some simple weekly response (an "okay" in the child's assignment book, for example) will usually suffice.

Reward effort, not result. "If you get all As and Bs next marking period, we'll take you to Disney World." That's a generous parental offer, but not a very good one. What's wrong? The child cannot control the result, cannot control the grades that the teacher gives. This kind of offer is a dangling carrot that may be unreachable. How about this offer? "When you can recite all your multiplication tables perfectly, I'll buy you a basketball." That's not likely to work either. Renata may lack the confidence that she can ever learn all the multiplication tables. Offering a reward for good results doesn't help the child discover how to accomplish the task. Success is more likely with a contract that spells out (and rewards) tasks that move the child toward the goal, such as making flashcards for practicing the tables, spending twenty minutes a day studying with the flashcards, taking a practice multiplication quiz twice a week, and so on.

Ask children why they got a low grade on a test, and you'll probably get one of these excuses: (1) "I'm just not a good speller" or "I can't do word problems." (In other words, lack of ability is blamed.) (2) "I'm not a good test-taker" or "I had a stomach ache that morning." (In other words, physical or emotional problems interfered.) (3) "The teacher didn't ask about the stuff I studied." (It was bad luck.) (4) "The test asked for facts that weren't even in the book." (It wasn't a fair test.) What's the real answer? The most likely reason for poor performance on a test is that the student didn't study enough. That's what we want children to realize. A contract that motivates children to put forth daily effort teaches not only subject matter but also the invaluable lesson that sustained effort brings satisfactory results. That's the most important academic lesson for children to learn.

Give the right reward at the right time. One reason that contracts fail is because something is wrong with the reward. First, the reward must be something the child really wants; otherwise it will not motivate effort. (The "right" reward may be money, a new game, an excursion with a parent, or permission to participate in a previously banned activity.) On the other hand, the reward should not be so great that it overrides the intrinsic satisfaction of doing a good job. Also, the younger the child, the shorter the time period should be between effort and reward. Point systems are one way to give small instant rewards that lead to a significant reward later.

Parents should be careful to create contracts that are extremely specific about the reward. Vague promises to give the child a vacation, a toy, or a night out with Mother can all lead to arguments and disappointments later. One mother we know found herself painfully seated on the horns of a dilemma because she had promised her daughter "an evening out with Mom and Dad, anywhere you want to go." Ten-year-old Nancy selected a sexually-explicit movie!

Reward rather than punish. We strongly recommend using rewards, not threats of punishments, as the motivating factor. Threats of punishment are likely to make children defiant and to set up parent-child power struggles. However, it is not punishment to require children to decrease time spent on other activities in order to make sufficient time for homework. Overscheduled children who do homework when they are exhausted are punishing themselves and must be stopped.

Stay within the limits of the contract. Suppose the contract stipulates that Ben will complete his math homework assignments on time. The parent may check the assignment book and the math paper to be sure that all the work is completed. But if the contract doesn't stipulate that all the answers must be correct and the paper must be neat, the parent cannot require correctness and neatness. The child has fulfilled the contract by putting time and effort into the work and is entitled to "payment" for that day's effort. Both parent and child must take the contract seriously and remain bound by the terms. (However, the contract can contain a clause stipulating that the parent will check a small portion of the work for accuracy before the remainder of the assignment is tackled.) If children find that their parents are using the contract as an excuse to oversee and criticize every aspect of their homework, the contract will not work. Parents need to remember that it is the teacher's job to determine whether the homework is of acceptable quality or not.

Renegotiate the contract. The contract is guaranteed to be successful if it begins with a level of achievement and effort that the child is capable of, comfortable with, and willing to agree to. However, progress requires frequent renegotiation to keep raising the amount and level of the work. When the teacher and parent are satisfied that the student is working fairly independently and at a satisfactory level, then it's time to consider phasing out the contract.

Don't create a contract to control a child. Yes, we want children to do their homework. It is important for kids to develop self-discipline, a sense of responsibility, habits of persistence, and organizational skills. Doing homework can help them develop in these ways. But parents should not use contracts to attempt to control or manipulate children into accepting the parents' standards of excellence, neatness, or achievement. Parents should guide, motivate, influence, and inspire their children, but they should not try to control every aspect of their lives. Students produce excellent work when they are interested in the subject matter and have confidence that their effort will produce good results. Contracts are useful to motivate children to master the major skills and gain the important information offered at each grade level. But a contract is unlikely to turn a B- student into a bookworm. Parents cannot inoculate their children with academic ambition by "buying" their efforts via a contract.

Don't force a contract upon a child. Most children respond enthusiastically to the suggestion of a contract. Even Arthur, who was terrified of swimming, agreed to take the plunge when a prize was offered. But defiant children, who may view contracts as just another form of adult efforts to manipulate them, may refuse to make a deal. In such cases parents should not despair. Defiance is usually a temporary state, and the contract idea may meet with approval next time it is suggested. However, a chronically defiant child or one who doesn't trust the parent to abide by the terms of the contract may continue to say, "No." In this case a parent might try an informal agreement, a trade-off. These kinds of agreements may appeal to kids who want to see their parents make some changes, too.

Agreeing to Agree—Informally

Informal agreements between an adult and a child can help a great deal to move the child forward academically. In these kinds of agreements there is no prize per se. But there is, nonetheless, a significant payoff. If the child agrees to make certain changes in behavior, the adult agrees to make changes too. Regarding homework, what do kids want from their parents? They want help when they need it, they want help that does not insult them, and they want freedom from parental urging to get the homework done. What do they want from teachers? They want homework that is not too difficult, too boring, or too long. What do parents want? In general, they want their kids to do their homework independently, without parental reminders, coaxing, supervision, or incessant intervention. What do teachers want? They want their students to progress, in part by doing homework assignments that help them advance. Keeping these desires in mind, it's not difficult to imagine what some workable trade-offs might be.

Joseph, a fourth grader, was a good math student but not a sufficiently fluent reader. In discussing this at a conference, his parent and teacher came up with this plan: Joseph's teacher would excuse him from some of the math practice homework (which he didn't really need) if Joseph would agree to read (anything he wanted) for a half hour a day and then write a brief report for his teacher summarizing what he read. Joseph stayed with this arrangement for the rest of the school year, happy to be free from the boring drill on math he already knew. When teachers are willing to take the time to individualize homework and negotiate with children in this manner, homework becomes a more valuable part of the student's academic progress.

Tia was too dependent upon parental help, so her mother suggested this: Tia had to begin taking careful notes in class, writing down whatever explanations and examples the teacher gave. She also had to spend ten minutes at home studying the examples in her notes and in the textbook. Then she had to try to do the assignment. Her mother would check the work, and if Tia didn't seem to "get it," then her mother would explain it to her. In other words, Tia was being encouraged to be more self-sufficient but with the reassurance that help would be there if necessary.

Ashley wants her father to read her essays and comment upon her ideas. She doesn't want him to launch into a long lecture on comma usage, something she hasn't studied much in school yet. Before her father reads the paper, the two of them can make an agreement: she will accept his negative comments about the logic and organization of her arguments; he will refrain from commenting upon other matters, such as spelling, punctuation, and penmanship. Adverse criticism must come in small, manageable doses; otherwise, it is too discouraging to be helpful. Perhaps some other time Ashley might humor her father by listening to his insights on the fascinating subject of comma usage.

We all know that children don't want their TV viewing interrupted by that dreaded question "Have you done your homework yet?" Parents feel obligated to ask but wish they didn't have to. Sometimes this problem can be solved by a trade-off agreement: Judy promises to complete her homework and show it to Mom or Dad by 8:15 every school night, and her parents agree not to ask that awful question anymore.

Informal agreements and contracts help parents and kids treat each other with greater respect. They also establish boundaries that cannot be crossed, thus circumventing angry shouting matches and tearful scenes of despair. Drafting an agreement helps both parties (parents and kids) take a step back and notice how they might be contributing to a homework problem and how they might solve it. If homework hassles are turning your home into a battlefield, try establishing a truce. No one need surrender. A contract is a win-win situation, giving both sides a victory.

5

Dealing with the Emotional Component

Emotional Interference

Emotions, moods, temperaments, and attitudes have a great effect upon learning. Positive feelings and attitudes—enthusiasm, ambition, curiosity, a love of knowledge in general, an intense interest in a particular field of study, confidence in one's ability—all these can enhance learning. One of the most powerful initial motivators for learning and achievement is a desire to win the respect and admiration of others: parents, teachers, mentors, or heroes. Children strive to be liked by and to be like the adults they admire. With time, the ideal becomes internalized; it motivates efforts to do well and to do good.

At school emotional upsets that disturb a child's concentration can be evoked by an overly critical teacher or hostile classmates. At home a child may be troubled by parental pressure to achieve, too much parental control, or, conversely, an insufficient amount of attention from preoccupied parents. Some children have the capacity to make good decisions and act appropriately even when upset; others can't. Let's look at some of the common emotional upsets surrounding homework and consider what parents can do to help, keeping in mind the following: first, a child's negative reaction to school-work is of concern only if it is a part of a *pattern* of behavior; second, no particular child is defined by any one label. Obviously, Terry may be anxious about math but confident about geography. Irina may be an eager art student but a procrastinating essayist. Sometimes a predominant attitude or behavior prevails, but even that will exist to a greater or lesser degree, depending upon the subject matter and the student's strengths and interests.

The Anxious Student

Anxious students are generally adequate or even good students. However, because of their anxiety, they may not enjoy the process of learning; they are too focused upon the outcome, worrying about getting a lower grade than they can tolerate or looking stupid to classmates and the teacher.

Tips for parents: First, realize that no student will be successful without some level of anxiety. As Renate and Geoffrey Caine point out in *Making Connections: Teaching and the Human Brain* (1991), "Occasional stress and anxiety are inevitable and are to be expected in genuine learning. The reason is that deep-level changes lead to a reorganization of the self, and that can be intrinsically stressful." Second, accept the fact that you cannot completely relieve your child's anxiety. Third, don't make your child's anxieties your own. It's easier for children to overcome their anxieties about schoolwork if their parents don't share them. (Just as a toddler won't cry much about a scraped knee if Mommy doesn't treat it as life-threatening.) Fourth, don't argue with your child about his or her fears. When Abraham complains that he can't do some academic work, it's as natural as breathing for a parent to offer a reassuring response such as, "Yes, you can. You're good at math." But it's the wrong response. That kind of "encouragement" only increases the child's anxiety. Now the child has an additional worry—about failing to reach parental expectations. A more helpful comment is "Keep working at it, and you'll get better." Fifth, suggest ways to break big jobs into a series of small tasks. Help the child work out a schedule indicating when and how each task will be handled. How do you eat an elephant? The answer is "One bite at a time." It's an important lesson to teach every child, but especially the anxious youngster.

The Pessimistic Student

Pessimistic children lack confidence in their ability to reach their goals. The result: a feeling of futility that saps the energy to try.

Tips for parents: A pessimistic child (like an anxious child) can't be talked out of his or her feelings. The more parents pooh-pooh the inadequacies the child feels, the more "evidence" the child will seek in order to "prove" his or her ineptness. Left alone, most pessimistic children will eventually come to a more accurate assessment of their own strengths and weaknesses. If this doesn't happen, effective "treatment" is the same as for the anxious student: break school assignments into manageable portions. Also, encourage kids to work on tough assignments when they are most alert. Then, as each part of the task is completed satisfactorily, point out the progress, giving the student reason for optimism.

The Highly Competitive Student

"So what's the problem?" some parents might ask, wishing their own children felt driven to be best in the class. It calls to mind this story of Los Angeles Dodgers pitching legend Sandy Koufax: After another of his stunning victories, Koufax was holding an ice pack on his chronically painful arthritic elbow. A sports writer standing nearby nodded toward it and said, "Too bad." Walter Alston, the Dodgers' manager, replied, "Yeah. I wish all my pitchers had that elbow." Most parents feel that way about the highly competitive student. They're quite content with this student despite the loss of sleep, complaining, and tension that may accompany the continuing struggle for academic superiority. Some parents do worry that their intense students are spending so much time on schoolwork that they are not leading a balanced life. But being academically competitive does not keep students from having friends and enjoying life. In fact, successful students are usually well-liked by peers, and they also derive a profound sense of satisfaction from their accomplishments. However, problems arise when academic ambition motivates cheating or an unwillingness to share knowledge and skills with classmates. The competitive child should also be able to work cooperatively with others and not look down upon those less capable.

Tips for parents: Encourage your child's ambition, but don't make it your own. Children shouldn't feel pressured to be top students because their parents expect them to be. Also, praise the academically successful child for other good qualities—especially interpersonal behavior, such as being considerate and respectful of others. Be sure that your good student understands that being a successful student is not all there is to being a successful person.

The Passive-Resistant (or Passive-Aggressive) Student

The term *passive resistance* has been associated with heroic public figures such as Mahatma Gandhi and Martin Luther King Jr., who protested evil laws by refusing to obey them. But used in a psychological sense, the term is not complimentary. It refers to an indirect way of expressing opposition through passivity and/or dependency. Passive-aggressive students do not directly refuse to do their schoolwork. In fact, they usually promise to do it. But then it doesn't get done, or it doesn't get done right, or it doesn't get done completely. Excuses are plentiful—a lack of supplies, a stomach ache, interference from a younger sibling, and so on and on. Passive-aggressive students may also daydream in class, ignore explanations, and then claim that the work is too difficult, beyond their comprehension.

Eventually the passive-aggressive student may give in and do the work, but very likely it will be a mess. Handing in the math problems on a torn, crumpled sheet of paper or writing the problems so closely together that the teacher can hardly read them—these tactics express in a passive way the child's anger or annoyance. "Okay, I'll do it, but not the way you want it," the child is saying silently, resisting conformity every step of the way. The teacher correctly interprets this messy work as a put-down and is insulted by it. The relationship between student and teacher deteriorates. Though passive-aggressive students often have good social skills, even a charming manner, because they continually disappoint their teachers and parents, they are viewed as annoying and untrustworthy. Then when they are not treated with the respect and trust accorded to other children, they become even angrier, more anxious, and, of course, even more passive-aggressive.

Passive-aggressive students do not admit to others and may not even admit to themselves that their behavior is a form of protest. When teachers and parents get angry with them, passive-aggressive kids are likely to say (and actually believe) that they are being treated unfairly.

Tips for parents: Parents may wonder why a child adopts passive-aggressive behavior. There are many possible reasons, one of which is a great deal of anxiety about aggressive feelings. However, the best initial route is not to get into long discussions with the child about the nature of and reasons for the behavior. Most important, parents (and teachers) should not get sucked into the game, should not expect the child to keep his promises about finishing schoolwork and then react with rage when the promise is broken. Often, if the adult refuses to get riled, the passive-aggressive student will give up the game. Matt, for example, repeatedly angered his fourth grade teacher with his "I don't have a pencil" line. But when he got into fifth grade, his teacher refused to scold him. To his "I can't find my pencil," she would respond calmly, "Then I guess you'll have to borrow one." In this classroom Matt's pencil soon stopped hiding from him.

Contracts often work well and win the cooperation of passive-aggressive students.

The Procrastinating Student

"I'll do it tomorrow." These are familiar words that parents hate to hear. As adults well know, tomorrow never really comes. When it turns into today, procrastinators are no more eager to do homework than they were the day before. What makes a procrastinator? It may be pessimism. ("I can't do it, so I won't shame myself by trying and failing.") It may be passive-aggressive behavior. In some cases it's simply that the child lacks the discipline to put work before play.

Tips for parents: Whatever the reason for the procrastination, children who put off schoolwork benefit from more structure. A household rule or contract that establishes a daily set time period for homework is needed. Remember that when children participate in the creation of a family rule or a contract, it is much more likely to work.

The Disorganized Student

What are some typical characteristics of a disorganized student? Many parents are painfully familiar with them. The assignment isn't written down correctly. Materials needed to do it are left at school. Directions at the top of the page are ignored. Ideas are developed illogically. Homework assignments are not completed and/or not turned in on time.

Why are children disorganized? Often disorganization is a way to resist and counter an order imposed by adult authority, usually a parent or teacher. In other words, it may be a form of passive resistance. But disorganization may also be the result of a learning disability, attention-deficit hyperactivity disorder, or simply study skill deficits not associated with any specific disability. Finally, homework may be disorganized when children don't understand the material.

Many parents deal with sloppy children by organizing things for them. This is commonplace at home and occasionally even extends to school. We've been told of one parent who comes to school periodically to straighten up her son's desk and locker! Of course, parental takeover such as this doesn't teach organization; it encourages disorganization.

Tips for parents: First, acknowledge that children may have more order than the adults in their lives realize. That is, the desk may look a mess, but the child knows where everything is. In this case there may be no need for rearranging. Second, don't expect more orderliness than is reasonable for the child's age. Third, let the child suffer the consequences of disorder. If Ellen can't find her pencil sharpener quickly, she'll miss some of the words on the spelling test and get a low grade. As a result, she'll learn that it pays to keep her supplies more neatly organized. At home too there can be unpleasant consequences when children can't find the possessions they want because everything is in disarray. After children see the disadvantages of disorder, they may be more open to suggestions about how to get organized. At this point a contract is a good additional motivator. Fourth, discuss homework assignments to be sure that students understand the information they are trying to organize. More tips on helping children get organized are discussed in Chapter 6.

The Unmotivated Student

"He has no motivation. He doesn't try. He doesn't care how he does in school. He doesn't seem to care about anything." What sort of a child is the parent describing? This may be a youngster with serious psychological or drug abuse problems, who is extremely withdrawn and socially isolated. It may be a child who has been so defeated by the school environment that the only path left open is a deep and thorough indifference. But more commonly, students who appear unmotivated, who seem to have no emotional involvement in school at all, may simply be resisting arbitrarily imposed motives and goals that parents and/or educators have forced upon them.

Tips for parents: Don't try to impose your view of accomplishment. Try to find out what the child's needs, desires, dreams, and goals are, and be responsive to these. Try a contract. If these techniques don't help, consider professional guidance.

The Daydreamer

"He wasn't listening. He was daydreaming again." Teachers and parents get exasperated when children tune them out and tune into their own private thoughts. Daydreaming can be another example of passive-aggressive behavior or a technique for dealing with anxiety or unhappiness. But parents should realize that virtually everyone daydreams to some extent, and that some daydreaming is valuable, helping the dreamer connect to his or her own innermost thoughts.

For a sympathetic portrayal of a chronic daydreamer, parents and kids should read *My Friend Flicka*, Mary O'Hara's beautiful novel about a boy whose frequent escapes into the world of his dreams make him unable to function well as a student or as a helper on his father's ranch. When his parents give him his own horse to raise and train, remarkable changes occur. Early in the novel Ken's hopes are fulfilled only in his daydreams. When the real world offers more possibilities, Ken becomes more attentive to reality. Those who enter Ken's world (via the book or the movie) get a better understanding of the daydreaming child.

Tips for parents: Daydreamers should not be punished, scolded, shamed, or even discouraged. One teacher we know tells her students to be *smart* daydreamers, by which she means that they should daydream at appropriate times and not when she is explaining the homework. When daydreams become a substitute for finding satisfaction in the real world, parents can help by steering a child toward a new interest that can lead to a sense of accomplishment and/or companionship. A pet, a new hobby, membership in a new group— any of these could help.

The Defiant Student

Defiant students can easily upset parents. In general, parents want their children to be obedient, to conform to the school rules, to do what the teacher says, and to turn in all the homework. But parents should realize that defiant students are, at least, emotionally invested in the school situation. They have expectations, frustrations, and reactions. They have the courage to be defiant. When defiance is nonviolent and only occasional, parents should allow children to suffer the consequences and learn from those experiences.

Here are two examples of defiant behavior that parents allowed to happen, and their children's world did not fall apart. Margaret, a sixth grader and an excellent and voracious reader, suddenly announced to her mother, "It's none of my teacher's business what I'm reading and whether I like it or not. I'm not writing any more book reports." Her mother pointed out that, if she didn't, she'd probably get a low grade in reading, and Margaret said she didn't care. Her mother didn't push the matter. Margaret turned in no book reports that marking period and got a low grade in reading. Having made her protest and disliking the result, she soon returned to more diligent homework habits.

Frank was a good student enrolled in a required (state mandated) high school course that he considered "dumb." Entitled Consumer Education, the course included assignments such as going to three different supermarkets to check the price of a can of peas. Frank simply didn't do this "shopping" assignment or the course workbook, which he also considered "silly." Other students in the course split up the assignments, exchanged answers, and made a pretense of doing the work. Frank, however, would not pretend. Finally, the somewhat sympathetic teacher made a deal with him: if Frank could get an A on the final exam, the teacher would give him a D (a low but passing grade) in the course. And that's what happened. The following year, when state regulations allowed it, Frank's school began giving a pretest to see if students needed a consumer education course. A great many tested out of this requirement. Frank was correct. The course was unnecessary for him and for many other students. He could have chosen another form of protest (perhaps letters to the local school board and the state board of education). Still, his act of direct defiance was passive resistance in the positive sense of the term.

Tips for parents: Don't quash every defiant response your child ever has. If we want children to be independent thinkers, we must expect occasional objection to and defiance of adult decisions. The trick is to encourage nondestructive, reasoned expressions of defiance in situations where the cause is worth fighting for. Students whose defiance disrupts school life or leads them to fail academically are, of course, going too far and need adult intervention.

Parents can also help angry kids by encouraging them to stop and think before acting, to make a list of possible responses and consider how each might affect them and others. If kids can be kept from acting upon anger immediately, they will probably choose actions less damaging to themselves and others.

The Withdrawn Student

The isolated child who doesn't feel accepted as part of the classroom social group is likely to be an apathetic, inattentive student. While most withdrawn students are not actually clinically depressed (that is, they do not have a mood disorder), their behavior suggests depression, and they may need psychological counseling.

Tips for parents: Try the homework buddy solution. Encourage the withdrawn child to invite a classmate (or even two or three) to come over after school to study or work on a school project. It's also a good idea to discuss this child's isolation with the teacher who can create classroom opportunities for group work and subtly steer a shy child into a supportive group situation.

The Perfectionistic (or Compulsive) Student

Perhaps no emotional need interferes with learning more than the need to be perfect. Perfectionism has nothing to do with being the best or even being good at something. Rather, it is about eliminating mistakes. In order to grow, students must be willing to try new endeavors, make mistakes, and learn from their mistakes. The perfectionist cannot do these things. The perfectionist repeats what is safe in a robotic fashion. If a teacher offers a correction or suggestion, the compulsive child cannot benefit from it. Instead of using the correction to improve, the compulsive child is devastated by it. These students deprive themselves of the joy of learning because they see every new learning experience as a threat to their self-esteem.

Tips for parents: First, recognize that this is a serious emotional problem for which the child may need professional help. Second, don't criticize the perfectionism. That blocks what the child considers the only safe path. (If the child can't avoid criticism by avoiding error, where else is there to turn?) Third, don't encourage perfectionism by overreacting to minor errors in a child's homework. It's not the parents' job to see that children turn in error-free homework. In fact, it's helpful for teachers to find out what their students didn't understand. It tells them what needs to be retaught.

When Emotional Problems Seem Serious

"How do I know if my child's emotional problems require professional help?" Parents who are unsure should talk to the teacher and other adults who have observed the child's behavior in the outside world with other children and with adults. School psychologists and social workers can sit in a classroom or stand around the playground and watch a particular child. They can also test a child whose behavior seems inappropriate to parents. In addition, at home parents can look for these four indicators of serious mental problems: (1) withdrawal and isolation; (2) extreme perfectionism; (3) frequent nonsensical or incomprehensible speech; and (4) a pattern of destructiveness (either self-injury or deliberate destruction of property). Of course, even if a child's behavior includes none of these four characteristics, if the parents feel unable to deal with the child's emotional excesses, there is no harm in seeking professional advice.

Michael Bloomquist's book *Skills Training for Children with Behavior Disorders* is an excellent reference for parents concerned about their children's emotional well-being. Chapters deal with such topics as helping children learn to follow rules, control anger, improve social skills, enhance academic skills, and understand and express feelings. Contracts are recommended, and the text includes sample behavior charts for tabulating progress.

Medications can be helpful for various emotional and attentional difficulties, but they are probably given to many children who could improve without them. Moreover, it is our experience that drugs help only when children understand that the medication is offered in support of their own commitment to improve. Medicated children must understand that the major ingredient leading to improved behavior is not in the pill but in their own effort.

Games Families Shouldn't Play

Parent-child interactions involving homework provide a multitude of opportunities for emotional stress. In many households manipulative games and power struggles abound. If any of the following homework games are played regularly in your home, clean house and throw them out. They accomplish no positive goals and are great sources of resentment. There are no long-term winners, and much can be lost.

Name of the Game:
"Me Too, You Too"

Object: The child uses homework as a way of monopolizing the parents' attention, forcing the parents to put as much time and effort into the homework as the child does.

Example: One mother of twelve-year-old fraternal twins describes their homework behavior as follows: "Bobby, assigned the task, could probably build a nuclear bomb without asking for help. Barry wants love, support, cola, cookies, and TV while doing the smallest assignment. Bobby is computer-independent. Barry wants me to push his fingers on the keys."

Outcome: Which twin is getting Mommy's goat? That's easy to tell. "Children will take up as much time as parents allow," one mother wisely observed. Children love and, in general, thrive on attention. But there are so many experiences that parents and kids can share. It's too bad if homework eats up most of their hours together. Perhaps Barry's mother could make a deal—if Barry did his homework alone and let mother do her own work, there would be time later for a game of checkers together.

Name of the Game:
"Guilt, Guilt, Who's Got the Guilt?"

Object: Either the parent or the child can initiate this game. The parent "wins" by making the child feel guilty about needing help and imposing upon the adult's valuable time. The child "wins" by making the parent feel guilty about lacking the time or ability to solve homework problems.

Example: In Lynne Sharon Schwartz's beautiful novel *Disturbances in the Field*, the main character's daughter comes home from school and says to her mother, "I need to do an experiment to weigh air for science. How do you weigh air?" The child expects the parent to know and deftly places the burden for finding the answer onto her mother's shoulders. Later, the mother gets a phone call from her friend who's a scientist, forgets to ask her friend the homework question of the day, and then feels guilty about forgetting. The busy mother then shifts the burden of responsibility to the father. It's a familiar homework scenario.

Outcome: Manipulative games that make a parent or a child feel guilty and inadequate do not enhance family relationships or the process of learning. Yes, parents should help when they can, but the ultimate responsibility for getting homework done is the child's. Parents need to be clear about the fact that they cannot (and should not) always drop their own lives instantaneously to help with homework.

Name of the Game:
"Mommy, Fix It" or "Daddy, Make It All Better"

Any problems at school or with homework? A parent intercedes to defend the child.

Object: The child "wins" by being as dependent as possible. The adult "wins" by proving himself or herself, again and again, the essential protector.

Outcome: The student is able to postpone taking initiative and developing her own strategies for coping with school problems.

Name of the Game: "Will the Real Student Please Not Stand Up?"

Object: The child's goal is to get the parent to come up with the idea for an essay, science project, etc. and perhaps even do most of the work. If the project works out well, the child takes credit. If it doesn't, the parent is blamed. Parents may also find this game appealing because it gives them a key role in the child's schoolwork.

Outcome: The child who is taking credit for work that the parent actually did is bound to feel guilty and inadequate because of this deceitful behavior.

Name of the Game: "Fight the Dragon"

Object: The teacher is the villain, an enemy to be crushed. For a parent the object may be to keep the child from bonding with another adult. For a child the goal may be a way to undermine the teacher's authority and escape from the teacher's control.

Outcome: One psychiatrist we know advises parents, "If you want your children to succeed in school, tell them the teacher is always right." This extreme point of view makes a worthwhile point: children need to get similar messages from their parents and their teachers. Otherwise, there is no clear, right path to follow. When parent and teacher battle, the child is usually the one that gets scarred.

Name of the Game:
"Follow in My Footsteps"

Object: The parent "wins" by turning the child into a clone and then taking credit for the child's achievement.

Outcome: The child has insufficient opportunity to develop his own talents and interests, feels stifled, and will eventually either rebel or, if remaining compliant, feel great resentment against the controlling parent. Either way, both parent and child lose this game.

Emotional Lessons—at School and at Home

Daniel Goleman's *Emotional Intelligence* stresses these two ideas: (1) people who can pause and think instead of acting purely on impulse are likely to be more successful and happier in all avenues of their lives; and (2) effective responses to problematic situations can be taught. Children get their earliest and most important "instruction" in emotional development at home before they even start school. But given the attention focused upon intra- and interpersonal skills by widely-read authors such as Howard Gardner and Daniel Goleman, plus the fact that so many students seem to lack these skills, some schools have taken on the task of teaching what is often called *emotional literacy*. Nowadays, classroom lessons teach kids how to manage stress effectively, resolve conflicts without aggression, and show kindness to others via compliments and consideration. In fact, says a *Time* article (September 29, 1997), "As many as 700 school districts across the country have instituted programs to nourish students' souls as well as their minds."

Of course, schools cannot train kids to control their emotions. No one can. Many emotions are fleeting; they come and go too quickly to control. The goal is not to stifle the emotion but to control the behavior that may result from various feelings, to raise the level of emotional and social competence. The first step is to help youngsters recognize their feelings. Goleman describes a first-grade lesson in which students use a "feeling cube" inscribed with words such as "sad" and "excited." The kids take turns rolling the cube and relating their personal experiences with various emotions. The goal: to help kids identify and express their own feelings and realize that other children have similar emotions.

In the intermediate grades, when peer relationships become critically important to youngsters, some schools offer lessons in properly channeling behavior when angry. In one classroom that Goleman describes, a poster of a stoplight is used as a metaphor for impulse control. Red means to stop and calm down before responding. Yellow is a reminder to identify the problem, set a goal, think of possible solutions to the problem, and consider the consequences of each possible solution. Green means select the best plan and try it. In another classroom that Goleman mentions, the teacher begins a discussion of emotions by asking her students to tell about a recent disagreement they had that worked out well. Instead of starting with generalizations, students begin in the world of real, specific experiences and move from there to develop abstract social and moral rules.

School districts that have tried emotional literacy programs are convinced that they have helped. At one school where students are suspended for fighting, the introduction of emotional literacy classes led to a precipitous drop in suspensions. Teacher evaluations of such programs indicate that students who have been involved in emotional literacy programs are better able to deal with their own emotions and with social relationships. Individual students have offered testimonials stating how programs of this sort taught them to handle their lives better. Moreover, Goleman points out that "emotional literacy programs improve children's *academic* achievement scores and school performance." Goleman refers to a study that indicates that school success is not predicted so much by academic knowledge and skills as by social and emotional factors—being able to curb impulses to misbehave, follow directions, ask the teacher for help when needed, and get along with other children.

Goleman also relates emotional literacy to the development of good character. "The bedrock of character is self-discipline," he says. "A related keystone of character is being able to motivate and guide oneself, whether in doing homework, finishing a job, or getting up in the morning." To be able to delay gratification, control and channel urges, put aside a self-centered focus and consider others—these are some of the elements of good character that we want children to learn.

Since the frontal lobes of the brain, which are critical to the control of behavior when emotionally aroused, continue to develop until about age eighteen, parents and schools have a wide window of opportunity in helping kids to mature emotionally and socially. Goleman believes that in the long run emotional intelligence is at least as important as IQ and explains, "At best, IQ contributes about 20 percent to the factors that determine life success, which leaves about 80 percent to other forces." These other forces include academic opportunities, social and economic status, emotional and social skills, and a bit of good luck. But students who understand themselves and others well are better equipped to make their own breaks.

As educators debate and experiment with the role of schools in cultivating good judgment about emotional matters, parents wonder what their role should be. Certainly they should not go overboard and encourage kids to continually take their emotional pulse. Jenny is that kind of kid. On the playground, instead of playing with classmates, she sidles over to the teacher to discuss the ebb and flow of her angry feelings. This excessive focusing on one's inner life is clearly not desirable.

Yet parents can and should be tuned in to their children's emotional stresses. Parents can teach their children emotional management in these ways: (1) by example (Like sponges, children tend to soak up what's around them. If their parents are emotionally intelligent, kids will learn from observation.); (2) by predictable, appropriate responses to their children's emotional needs; and (3) by brainstorming with kids about how to handle specific emotionally-charged social situations.

In "treating" their children's emotional ailments, parents want to be therapeutic, not toxic. How to do this? Remember that discipline (intelligent, consistent structure) is what's needed, not punishment. In working out whatever changes children need to make, negotiation and compromise with the child must be part of the plan. Parents cannot and should not try to protect kids from ever making mistakes. Children should learn from their mistakes, find ways to rectify the damage, forgive themselves for errors, and avoid letting their mistakes keep them from feeling good about the many things they have done right. Emotional health requires that children respect themselves. Parents can help their children achieve that goal by treating their kids with love and respect.

6

Clearing Homework Hurdles

To Help or Not to Help?

Diane G. admits to being two different people in one body. "As a teacher, I tell parents to allow their children to make mistakes and learn from the consequences. But, functioning as a parent, I'm up at 2 A.M. helping my daughter Melanie get a paper finished." Diane is a typical parent. She doesn't want her child to be unhappy; she doesn't want her child to experience the pain of failure. So she rescues Melanie from the consequences of her procrastination and poor time management. This is, in the long run, a disservice to the child.

These days, parents are confused by conflicting advice regarding their children's academic life. They're told that they should be involved but, then again, they're warned not to take over the student's academic responsibilities. Sometimes it's a tough call for parents to know when to intervene and when to back off. Moreover, parents don't always know how to teach or how to do the work. Some of what kids learn in school today their parents never learned or have long forgotten. Some parents are not able to help much because of their limited knowledge of English. In households with only one parent or two employed parents, there may be very little time for helping kids with schoolwork. These situations do not doom children to academic failure. Children with positive attitudes toward learning can be resourceful and find whatever help they need.

Still, when assistance is needed, most parents want to help— especially when they're asked to get involved by either the teacher or the child. If the child seems to need more individual attention than the teacher is able to give, is there anything wrong with the parent providing academic assistance? In most situations help is helpful. But parents need to be cautious about excessive or continual homework involvement. There are three possible negative outcomes: the child may (1) become dependent upon parental help; (2) get the unintended message that she's unable to do schoolwork independently; or (3) substitute at-home teaching for careful listening and hard work in class. Too much help may produce a child like Sarah, who chides her father thusly: "You weren't home to help me last night, so I couldn't do my math homework." By the following week Sarah might be telling her father, "I failed the math test. You didn't teach it right."

One way to guard against long-term dependency and a shifting of responsibility to the parent is to put a limit on the amount of tutoring that will be given. Dad can say, "I'll spend a half hour an evening with you on algebra this week, but by next week let's limit our sessions together to twice a week." If, after a few weeks, algebra is still difficult for Sarah, Dad should not get roped into becoming her semester-long algebra tutor. Instead, parent and child together should try to determine why this homework problem is ongoing and what the student can do about it.

How Much Homework Is Just Right?

How much time your child spends on homework each night is affected by several factors: the pace at which your child works, the specific assignment, the grade level, the homework policies of the teacher and the school, and parental attitudes and expectations regarding homework within your community. Difficult as it is to generalize about homework quantity, if we look at the recommendations of professional educators and educational organizations, we find pretty much what we expect—short homework assignments are suggested for the primary grades and gradually increasing amounts as children get older. For example, one general rule of thumb for homework length says to add ten minutes for each grade level, as shown in the chart below.

According to a federally funded report entitled "How Important Is Homework?" the National Parent Teacher Association (PTA) and the National Education Association (NEA) suggest homework amounts similar to those listed above: for kindergarten through third grade, no more than twenty minutes per day; for fourth through sixth grades, twenty to forty minutes. For higher grades, no specific figures are given, since the quantity depends upon the specific subjects and program the student is enrolled in.

"Only fifteen minutes of homework a day!" surprised parents may say. "So, in the primary grades, parents don't get involved much." Wrong. In fact, the parental role in academics is probably most important in these first school years, as indicated in the next section.

Grade Level	Amount of Homework Per Day
first	10 minutes
second	20 minutes
third	30 minutes
fourth	40 minutes
fifth	50 minutes
sixth	60 minutes
seventh	70 minutes
eighth	80 minutes
high school	1½ to 3 hours

Homework Help in the Primary Grades

Some children need more help than others in making the transition from carefree kid to conscientious student. During these early school years parents should focus upon helping their youngsters develop attitudes and habits that will help them become successful learners. Here are some things you can do:

- Show your child that his school life is of interest to you. Ask about what happened at school each day, and really listen to the answer.
- Look at the material your child brings home each day. Discuss any notes from the teacher or the school. Look at homework papers. Ask your child if he knows how to do them and offer help getting started if he's not sure. Look at corrected homework, too, and ask your child if he understands the corrections. If not, take time to both explain and practice the concept.
- Is your child excited about what she learned at school today? Does she want to come home and duplicate the lesson, "teach" it to you? That's great! No matter how busy you are, make time to play the student role.
- At the beginning of the school year, discuss with your child and reach agreement as to an appropriate time of day and place for doing homework. When a particular time and location is associated with studying, it's easier to get started and to concentrate.
- Display and encourage positive attitudes toward homework. (Kids are more likely to do it if it brings pleasant experiences.) Praise your child for remembering to do her homework, for completing it, and for doing a good job. Help your child to recognize what new skill or information the homework has given her and what academic progress she's making. ("Now you know how to add any two digit numbers!")
- Observe your child at work, and make suggestions about easier, better techniques. For example, written homework should

---

Homework Reminder Sheet

Date: _____

My homework for today is:

_____

_____

_____

Student's signature: _____

Teacher's initials: _____

Parent's signature:_____

This kind of quick communication between home and school can help kids develop the homework habit.

Parents of forgetful kids should also set aside a time in the early evening for getting ready for school the next day. Everything that needs to go to school with the child—books, homework papers, backpack, a show-and-tell item, a permission slip for an upcoming school trip, lunch money, etc.—should be put in one place and in the same place every evening.

Finally, remembering can be encouraged by incentives such as a "star" chart or a contract offering a specific reward. For younger children a popular reward is often a special outing alone with a parent or the chance to stay up a little later than the usual bedtime.

"I'm not in the mood." Some kids, when they walk out of the school building, want to shut the door on academics for the day. They have trouble getting started on homework. Household routines or rituals can help to get kids psychologically in tune to open their textbooks. Writing in *Parents* (August 1997), Noelle Fintushel explains what turns a routine into a ritual. It is "the attitude we bring to it, the feeling that what we are doing has a value in and of itself." Rit-

be done at a table or desk rather than while sprav
bed or sitting cross-legged on the floor. When the
is supported, the writer gets less fatigued and the
neater. Also, observe how your child holds a pe
and offer suggestions when needed. However, a
how and where to do homework is best given *be*
begins to concentrate upon the work itself. Don't
child in the middle of multiplying with comments
ber formation.

- To teacher-assigned homework, add family activit
  your child using academic skills such as readin
  spelling, counting, and measuring. Parents of prir
  children should try to read with them every evenin
  upon both decoding and comprehension. Mastery
  these skills does not guarantee mastery of the ot
  children, called *hyperlexic*, decode very well at an ea
  have limited understanding of what they're "read
  questions and discuss the content to be sure that yo
  reading ideas, not just words. For more sugge:
  improving reading skills, see Chapter 12.
- Show pride in your young child's work by displaying
  nently in your home—on a family bulletin board or h
  wall.

Homework hurdles exist even for children in the primar
Let's talk about some typical problems and solutions:

"I forgot." The homework doesn't get home, doesn't get
doesn't get back to school. "I forgot" is the common explana
excuse. Early in a child's school career, parents want to conve
student the idea that homework is important and that the im
adults in his life care about its completion. The chronic f
needs help developing strategies for remembering. Primary
children usually don't have an assignment notebook, but th
effect can be achieved with a homework reminder sheet tha
parent and teacher sign (until the child no longer needs this cl
Here's a simple sample:

uals can be tied to what happens before, during, or after homework sessions. In some households a particular family activity always precedes homework time. (It may be reading the comics together, playing catch, walking the dog, phoning grandma, or exchanging anecdotes about the adventures of the day.) In other households study time itself is ritualized. Everyone in the family gathers in the same area (around the dining room table or in the living room or family room) and works on a quiet activity. Adults can do their own "homework"—reading the newspaper, paying bills, and so on—while the kids do school assignments. For children just starting out as students, it may seem punitive to be sent to their room to study alone while the rest of the family is watching TV and chatting. It's easier to be quiet and studious when that behavior is being modeled by others and when the child doesn't feel that homework is causing him to miss out on family fun. A family ritual can also be an activity that follows study time: enjoying a story, snack, card game, or computer game together. Thus, the ritual serves as an immediate mini-reward for completing homework as well as an opportunity for family members to share pleasures.

"I'm just not good at school." How to avoid this scary homework hurdle? Parents (with guidance from teachers) need to step in *early* to help a child who's falling behind. Some children are distracted by the classroom environment and don't pay attention well in school. Some kids just need more practice. Some have neurological difficulties that make learning more of a struggle. (See Chapter 13 for information about special needs students.) When the teacher recommends extra practice at home, parents must do everything possible to hide any feelings of anxiety from the child. The young student must get the message that the parent has confidence in the child's capacity to learn. Moreover, a parent should try to make tutoring sessions enjoyable. Busy parents should avoid communicating the idea that doing schoolwork with their child is an infringement upon their valuable time. After all, what could be more important than helping a child learn to read or count? Early, effective intervention is important before a student concludes, "I'm a bad reader," "I'm lousy in math," or "I'm just dumb." To help a child who needs more practice in basic skills, look to advice from the teacher, materials in teacher-parent stores, computer programs, instructional videos, and, if necessary, a tutor or learning specialist recommended by the school.

The Intermediate Grades and Beyond: Familiar Complaints

In Chapter 5 we dealt with emotional problems that cause homework difficulties. But the reverse is also true: homework difficulties create emotional reactions. Of course, parents and educators want kids to be emotionally invested rather than apathetic about their school-work. But what kinds of emotions? Ideally, adults hope that home-work will generate enthusiasm, curiosity, and, when completed, a sense of accomplishment. But we also know, from questionnaires that students completed for us, that homework is often a highly stressful experience for children. They're overwhelmed when there's too much, annoyed when it's boring, insulted when it's too easy, angry when it's unclear, frightened when they feel they should know how to do it but they don't, and nervous when a critical parent is about to check the results of their efforts. When children are upset and feel that they can't handle the situation, a calm parent with an appropriate suggestion can save the day.

Let's look at four general areas of homework complaints that parents hear most often, and find some solutions for them.

"It's too much."

"I can't do all this" is a common complaint especially when students have different teachers for different subjects and longer homework assignments not due the following day. Students can create this prob-lem by procrastinating until the evening before the due date or by obsessing over work and giving it more time than the teacher expects. In other words, "It's too much" is usually a time management problem. When there's more work than time, kids can learn to set priorities, to use the time available to do the assignment that's due first or that's most important.

So it's an hour past bedtime, and the homework is far from completed. What should the parent do? Close up the homework shop for the night. Children should not stay up long past their usual bedtime to finish homework. Then they will be tired the next day and unable to concentrate in school. It is better for them to do as much as can be done by their usual bedtime and then get to sleep. The child can write a note to the teacher explaining why a particular assignment wasn't completed on time and requesting an extension of time. Of course, this kind of request should not have to be made often. Hopefully, the development of time-management strategies will avoid frequent recurrences of the "It's too much" crisis.

The first step in effective time management involves analyzing where a student's time disappears to and where more study hours can be found. When Dan complained that he never had enough time to get his homework done, his parents encouraged him to write down, for a few days in a row, what he actually did during his after-school and evening hours. In his case a lot of time was being spent on TV shows, computer games, and phone conversations. Dan didn't want to curtail too much of his fun, so when he looked for more study time, he found some in "dead" time. He decided that he could work on his spelling words while in the car being driven to his swim classes. Maria, after looking at her schedule of extracurricular activities with her parents, reluctantly agreed that—between ice skating and tap dancing and girl scouts and religious school—she didn't have enough time left for homework. The next step was for Maria to figure out, on average, how much time she needed for homework each evening and to eliminate enough other activities to free up that time. Children with a lot of interests need to learn that they can't do everything—at least not all in the same semester.

Once a child has a good sense of what his commitments are, it's a good idea to work out a daily schedule. Not every child needs this, but it will help most. The schedule should not be imposed upon the child but negotiated with him. Some children don't want to do homework immediately after school. They need a period of socializing or physical activity first. Other kids cannot enjoy playing until they know their homework is done, so they prefer to get right to work after school. Some children prefer to do homework in half-hour chunks of time; others, once they get into it, can concentrate for longer periods and don't want to be interrupted until the task is done. Children need to make their own schedules. Parents can help by introducing them to the concept of planning. It may, of course, be somewhat different on different days of the week. It should include a set time for homework, household chores, recreation, dinner and snacks, and bedtime preparation. There should be an agreed-upon bedtime for all school children through junior high school.

Another aspect of time management is planning ahead when additional demands upon one's time come up. If Maria has an ice-skating show coming up that will tie up her entire weekend, she may need to revise her schedule to fit in more weekday study time. When a longer assignment is given in advance, encourage your child to use his or her personal calendar to write down the due date and some "do" dates.

"The essay is due Friday, so I'll do it Thursday," Tim says. Sounds fine, except that by Thursday there may be extensive homework in another subject. An adult understands that life is less worrisome when assigned work is done as soon as possible. Kids may need to be reminded of this. Why wait until Thursday when there's time to write the essay on Tuesday? By Thursday the child may have a cold or be invited to a friend's house. Some children learn to plan ahead only after they've had to miss out on fun because of postponed schoolwork. But who wouldn't prefer to enjoy the pleasurable rewards of successful planning?

Timing is especially important when the homework assignment is to produce a piece of writing. Good writing requires rewriting, and successful editing cannot be done immediately after a paper is completed. A two-day interval between writing and editing allows the author to reread his or her own work as if someone else had produced it. The creative eye is replaced by the critical eye. One of the most valuable homework tips that parents can give kids is to finish a writing project early, put it away for a few days, then take it out and read it aloud (or read it silently but slowly). When time is not an issue, a paper can even be reread a few times—once to see if the ideas are logically developed and a second time to check mechanics such as spelling and punctuation. When students ask "What can I read to improve my writing?" the best answer is "Read what you have written." That can be done if students plan ahead.

If the problem of too much homework cannot be solved by effective time management, talk to your child's teachers about it. If teachers hear the same comment from many parents, they may be convinced to cut back a bit or try to schedule assignments and tests so that work doesn't "bunch up" so much.

"What am I supposed to do?"

At 7 P.M. Joey took out his geography worksheet with every good intention of doing it. But, looking at all those maps and signs, he didn't know what to do. Whose fault? It may be Joey's. Maybe he didn't pay attention when the teacher explained. It may be the teacher's fault if she didn't explain it well. It may be the fault of a poorly designed worksheet with ambiguous or incomplete directions. Unless "I don't understand what to do" is a nightly complaint, parents shouldn't assume that the child is to blame. At any rate, in the midst of a homework crisis, parents shouldn't concern themselves with assigning blame. The focus should be on finding a *solution to the problem.*

What are the options here? First of all, the child can call a classmate for an interpretation of the work. (Every child should have the phone numbers of a few classmates to call for consultation. In some schools this idea is formalized into a homework partner system.) Note that we are *not* saying that the parent should call another parent. It is the child's homework, and the child should be resourceful about clarifying the assignment.

Suppose Joey's friends aren't home. What then? Parents must avoid getting engulfed in the child's momentary hysteria. A decision must be made: do nothing or do something? Probably the decision to do something is the better one. At least it shows the teacher that the child put some thought and effort into the assignment and did not just ignore or forget about it. Joey can do what he thinks the paper asks him to do. He can then attach a note to the teacher saying that he wasn't sure about what was wanted so he went with his best guess. Another possibility: Joey can do a different but closely related task of his own invention to get some practice working with the material assigned. Chances are, if Joey couldn't understand the assignment, many of his classmates couldn't either. Much homework hysteria over confusing assignments becomes a dead issue the next day when the teacher realizes that the assignment didn't "work."

Sometimes parents need to help students dispel anxiety when they cannot do exactly what the teacher assigned. Some kids fear a teacher's disapproval and may need to be reassured that teachers are reasonable people who will listen to an explanation.

"I need an idea."

Brainstorming time. Your child is in need of an idea for a science fair project, an essay, or a social studies paper. You are asked to (perhaps even expected to) come up with a great suggestion. Given the danger of family feuds and hard feelings inherent in this homework crisis, we've compiled a list of guidelines, suggestions for suggesters, if you will.

- Try to make more than one suggestion so the child can consider options.
- Focus upon the child's interests and experiences, not your own. For example, "Perhaps, since you're such an avid bike-rider, you might want to do a science fair project that compares different types of bicycles."
- Make general suggestions that the child can then make more specific. For example, "Maybe one of the Civil War sites we visited last summer would be a good topic for your history paper."
- If your child decides to use one of your suggestions, don't get overly involved in its development or show disappointment if the project doesn't turn out as you conceived of it. The child will develop your idea in his own way; that's as it should be.
- If your child decides not to use one of your suggestions, don't

be disgruntled. Show an interest in whatever topic the child ultimately chooses to work on.

- Admit your own limitations. If you have no ideas, refer your child to another, better qualified adult who might be able to help.
- Remember that it's not a parent's responsibility to come up with ideas for school projects. Don't feel guilty if you have to toss the ball back into the child's court. If your child then tells you that Helen's parents came up with a super idea for Helen's science project, the wise response is a cheery "That's nice."
- With a parental push in the right direction, kids *can* find their own ideas. For writing projects, encourage brainstorming aloud with a friend or family member or free association writing on the topic (just jotting down random thoughts continuously for several minutes, without regard to logical order or writing mechanics). For computer help with idea hunts, supply your child with an inexpensive paperback entitled *The Ultimate On-Line Homework Helper* by Marian Salzman and Robert Pondiscio. It tells kids how to find all kinds of homework assistance, including ideas for science fair projects.

"It's too hard."

"It's too hard" means "I don't know how to do it." When students do not understand concepts, parents have an opportunity (notice that we did not say *an obligation*) to become tutors. It's not a role parents should play night after night, like an actor cast in a long-running show, but it is a role parents can step into on an emergency basis, something like an understudy. For parents who are not professional teachers, here are our suggestions for making an occasional parent-child tutoring session successful:

- Find out specifically what is causing the child difficulty. Exactly what doesn't he understand? Don't try to teach beyond what is being asked.
- Ask if the student knows the goal of the assignment. If not,

consult the text and try to determine what the goal is, describe your interpretation to the child, and see if you can both agree upon what outcome is desired.

- Find out what the student already understands about the work. (No need to review subtraction without borrowing if it is only borrowing that's a mystery to the child.) Praise the child for a good understanding and clear explanation of what is already known.

- Begin instruction at an appropriate level considering the child's current knowledge and stage of development.

- Talk as little as possible. Listen as much as possible. (Listening shows respect for the learner and also helps the tutor adjust explanations to fit the learner's level of comprehension.) Ask questions and allow the student to explain what has been taught up to that point. The learning process should be one of "assisted discovery," says Lev Vygotsky, the brilliant Russian psychologist and early childhood educator. The more your student takes control of the tutoring sessions, the more she will understand and retain.

- Don't try to fake it. Children know anyway. (On our questionnaires about homework, one child wrote that he was least happy when his mother helped him with math because "she doesn't understand centimeters.") If you don't understand something, don't waste your child's time and your own. It will only make both of you angry. If you can't help, then help your child find real help elsewhere.

- Don't "lose your cool" and become angry if your student doesn't "get it." You won't be asked for help again if you shame your child because she is confused.

- Review and involvement are important keys to retention. One way to review is through role-playing. Take on the role of the befuddled student, and let your child explain the lesson to you. Ask questions—some stupid ones and some challenging ones—and see if "teacher" can field them.

- Know when to stop. Avoid recreating the scene where the father goes on and on about the water cycle, and the son, head in the palm of his hand, falls asleep. One good stopping point is when the child seems to feel comfortable and confident about the work. However, if the tutoring session isn't going well, that's also a good time to stop. You may both need a rest. The next day, at an earlier hour, you may have a better

---

Parent/Tutor Grading Scale

How good a tutor were you? Give yourself 0–3 points for each statement, with a 3 indicating behavior closest to the statement.

_____ 1. I listened more than I talked.

_____ 2. Everything I said related to the immediate learning task.

_____ 3. I didn't say anything that made my child feel bad, guilty, or stupid. (I didn't make any statements beginning with "Why didn't you . . . ?")

_____ 4. I praised effort and/or comprehension.

_____ 5. We reviewed concepts and methods periodically.

_____ 6. At the end of the tutoring session, my student seemed more confident about being able to do the work.

_____ 7. My students said, "Thanks!"

Total score : _____ Grade: _____ Perfect score (and perfect tutor): 21 points

Grading scale: A = 18–21; B = 16–17; C = 13–15; D = 11–12. (There are no failures. You get a passing grade for trying.)

---

idea of how to explain the material, and your child may be more alert and catch on more quickly.

Sometimes work that is too hard for children is also too hard for their parents. The student may need outside help. This doesn't necessarily have to cost a fortune. There may be books, videos, or computer programs that can teach a concept a child somehow didn't get from class, and these teaching materials may be available from a school or local library. Hiring a tutor is another option. Before hiring a tutor you don't know, be sure to ask for and check references. Then, before the tutoring sessions begin, discuss the goals and ask for an estimate of how many sessions will be needed to reach these goals. If your child needs help in a particular subject, don't wait until a week before finals to hire a tutor. Get help as soon as a problem becomes apparent. Tutoring can be quite expensive but it doesn't have to be. The school may be able to recommend, instead of a professional teacher, an older student who will charge much less and may provide the additional benefit of being a positive role model that the student can identify with. Also consider friends and relatives. People are often flattered to be asked and willing to give free help if it doesn't place too great a demand upon their time. With an older child parents can suggest tutoring sources and encourage the youngster to follow up with the phone calls or school inquiries. That's teaching resourcefulness.

How Else Can Parents Help?

Let's review some ways parents can help by what they *don't* do.

1. Never do the child's homework. The child doesn't learn from that and must also deal with the guilt of the deceit.
2. Don't be a broken record repeatedly reminding your child to do homework. There should be a schedule including a set homework time.

3. Don't check on homework completion. This should be done only on a short-term basis if your child's teacher has indicated that your child is a homework avoider. As soon as possible, return this responsibility to the student.

4. Don't make it a habit to correct the errors after your child has completed homework. Occasionally your child may request this kind of proofreading for an important paper or a new and confusing math lesson. But on a regular basis the student should check his or her own work. That is part of the job of doing homework.

5. Don't make judgments about the overall quality of your child's work. If you say it's a great essay and the teacher gives it a B, the student is likely to feel disappointed, even cheated. If you say, "Tear it up and start over," you may be wrong. Parents are usually more severe and less appropriate critics of kids' work than teachers are. If your child asks for your reactions to a writing assignment, rather than giving an overall evaluation, praise or suggestions for change should be specific: "I liked the way you tied everything together in the last paragraph." "This example really clarifies your point." "Perhaps this paragraph should be earlier in the essay." "I didn't understand this sentence."

Now let's turn to what parents *may* do. In the day-to-day effort to lead children toward successful homework completion, parents might want to use the following helpful tips:

Provide a satisfactory environment for doing homework.

Obviously, children need a suitable place to work and to keep their school supplies. Suitable means comfortable and well lit. It may or may not mean quiet, depending upon the child's personal style. (Some children find silence and isolation more distracting than family hubbub.) If household space allows, students find it helpful to have their own desk with their own school supplies that no one else in the family touches. Giving children their own work space and tools sends a message that their schoolwork is important.

React appropriately, promptly, and predictably to your child's academic efforts.

Children want the approval of the important adults in their lives. When their academic efforts and progress bring attention and praise, they are encouraged to continue in that direction. When kids fall behind in school, someone at home should notice and care and help devise a plan for improvement. Parents should have reasonable expectations about their children's academic efforts and achievement, and children should know what those expectations are.

Praise effort, not innate ability.

Don't keep telling your child how smart he is. Instead, praise effort and point out accomplishment. ("You've been reviewing for your test for over an hour. I'm proud of all the hard work you're putting into this" or "You see, you did it!") According to a study by Henderson and Dweck (1990), students who enter junior high school with the belief that they have done well in school because of their innate ability are more vulnerable to academic difficulty and discouragement than students who believe that intelligence comes from studying a lot. Children who attribute their academic success to inborn brain power, who consider themselves smart because they have always been able to understand quickly and do their schoolwork easily, may be headed for trouble as the work gets harder. After all, students who attribute their successes to innate ability must also consider their failures to be due to a lack of ability. What can they do about that? Morison and Brady (1994) comment upon the Henderson-Dweck study in *Homework: Bridging the Gap*, pointing out that children who consider intelligence a fixed trait want to prove they have the trait. As a result, they may be less willing to take risks to try to learn something new, and they are more easily discouraged by a difficult challenge.

Encourage self-regulation.

In an Australian study on homework self-regulation, researcher Pamela M. Warton reported some interesting statistics. Among the second graders she interviewed, only 23 percent felt that they should do their homework because it was their responsibility. They were more likely to do it because "Mum might be angry" if they didn't. However, by sixth grade, 67 percent of children were thinking along these lines: "It's my homework, so it's my responsibility to remember to do it." This study suggests that parents need to make clear to their younger children that they expect homework to be done. Eventually, this expectation will become internalized by the students, and reminders should disappear. Many parents, the study shows, continue in the role of regulators after their children are able to be self-regulators. That's a bad idea.

Be knowledgeable about your child's school life.

Is your child progressing satisfactorily in school? Specifically, what is she learning this year? You should know. Attend school meetings for parents to learn about the curriculum goals for each academic year and become acquainted with the school resources and staff. Pay attention to your child's standardized test scores to be sure that she's mastering the important skills and knowledge for each academic level.

Know when to contact the teacher.

If homework hurdles of any type last continually for more than a week, make an appointment to see the child's teacher(s). Children who are capable of dealing with school difficulties themselves do so. If they don't, chances are they can't. The parent's assertiveness models behavior that the child may be able to emulate next time around. Parents should not sit around and wait, hoping school difficulties will go away by themselves. Most teachers deal with twenty-five or more students each day and don't always notice when one of them gets "lost." Alert the teacher to your child's difficulties, and work with the teacher to find home and school solutions.

Encourage the right attitude about being wrong.

"What an interesting error!" Mr. H. tells one of his students. This teacher values mistakes, realizes that they can enable both teacher and learner to find out where the thinking process has gone awry and correct it. This teacher also knows that when students try something new, they will make mistakes. Eric Zorn, a *Chicago Tribune* columnist, makes this point: "Those who are afraid to fail will coast through life and never come close to their potential. Failure—honest failure despite effort—is an underrated teacher and motivator as well as a sign that one is striving at close to full capacity." Zorn quotes a Nike commercial in which Michael Jordan, Chicago Bulls' basketball star, says the following: "I've missed more than 9,000 shots in my career. I've lost almost 300 games. Twenty-six times I've been trusted to take the game-winning shot and missed. I've failed over and over and over again in my life. And that is why I succeed."

This chapter has come full circle. We began with Diane's advice: allow children to make mistakes. We conclude by urging parents to think of mistakes as an inevitable and *necessary* part of learning and growing. As you assist your child in discovering and using new knowledge, remember that academic struggles can be quite scary— like leaping off a diving board that keeps getting higher and higher. As a parent you want to help kids realize that the water is warm, the dunking is fun, and, when needed, you're there to help them navigate successfully in the deep water.

7

Taming Testing Terrors

Test Anxiety: A Student and Parent Affliction

In a 1997 legal case a medical student took his school to court in an effort to get special considerations (such as unlimited time on tests) because of what he considered his disability—test anxiety. The judge decided the case against him and advised him to find another solution, such as studying more. Test anxiety may not be considered a disability in the courtroom, but it certainly can be disabling in the classroom. No question about it, fears can interfere with test performance. Some kids thrive on tests, find them just another opportunity to demonstrate how much they know. Other students react to every test day as if it were Judgment Day.

Whether students like it or not, assessment is essential. It's necessary to find out who knows what. Although there is a trend toward using portfolios (collections of students' work) for evaluation, especially for writing courses, most assessment comes in the form of a test. Test scores can affect a school's rating, a child's grades, and a student's eligibility for gifted or honors programs. In high school opportunities for awards, scholarships, and acceptance by colleges all depend in large part upon test scores. Kids learn quickly that test scores are important, so it's not surprising that test anxiety is a common ailment.

Nerve-wracking as it is, American schools seem to be heading for an increase in testing. President Clinton and several state governors vigorously support the development of national curriculum standards and state or nationwide tests to assess student achievement in core subjects. According to an article in *Business Week* (June 30, 1997), these kinds of tests seem to promote learning. Analysis of data from the Third International Mathematics & Science Study, which in 1994 and 1995 tested seventh and eighth graders from thirty-nine countries, showed that students from countries with mandatory standardized exams performed, on average, a grade level higher on both subjects tested (math and science). Studies of Canadian students have also shown that students required to take standardized exams seem to learn more.

So testing, it seems, is here to stay. What can parents do to help curtail the headaches and heartaches it causes? First of all, don't be a test-anxious parent. Don't let your comments or behavior suggest to your child that you're worried about the test outcome. Remember, one test does not a future make. Parents should be especially careful not to assume that a standardized achievement test is a true summation of their child's abilities and/or potential. High test scores do not guarantee a successful and happy future, and many average students develop into outstanding adults. In his book *Schools of Hope*, Douglas H. Heath (professor emeritus of psychology and well-known consultant on education and youth) points out, "Success requires a variety of personality strengths that achievement and aptitude tests just don't measure." These include "imaginativeness, judgement, inductive skill, reflectiveness, and organizational and synthetic ability." In addition, he points out, these tests don't measure character strengths important for success, such as "curiosity, doggedness, and the maturity necessary to do well in one's work." Heath asks his reader to imagine preparing for and taking a multiple-choice test about the history of Idaho or Pennsylvania. To do well, what traits does the test-taker need? Here are just some of the qualities that Heath lists: "some *curiosity* about the state; *persistence* in reading the boring text; *accuracy* in taking notes; *thoroughness* in preparation; *judgement* about what is and is not important to learn; . . . *resilience* to keep going when not able to answer the first three questions; ability to *tolerate anxiety* when blanking out on the fourth." Parents can do much to encourage these traits in their children, thereby helping kids accomplish what Heath urges: integrating "the maturation of mind with that of character and self."

Children can't test better than their abilities or knowledge allow, but they can easily test worse. A child who's tired, hot, hungry, distracted by noise, in a bad mood, worried, etc., may do worse on Thursday than he would have done the preceding Monday. On standardized tests children who are careless may mark their answers in the wrong place. On the other hand, children who are very careful may not work fast enough. Of course, children should not be scolded or shamed because of low test scores. Nor should parents make a great deal of fuss over high scores, thereby pressuring the student with the burden that his parents will expect such high scores forevermore or giving the student the impression that he is loved and valued only because he's smart.

Suppose you're not anxious about the upcoming test, but your child is. Realize that test anxiety is not necessarily bad. The best students tend to be anxious about tests because they care so much about doing well. And that's good. But some students' emotions go far beyond ordinary anxiety. They feel persecuted by tests. In a testing situation they feel helpless and hostile. Emotions this strong are likely to have an adverse effect upon performance. For kids with real testing terror, more experience with tests is helpful. Practice tests can decrease anxiety since the unknown is always scarier than the known. Moreover, practice give students an opportunity to develop coping strategies. Before a major test younger kids can practice with a quiz written by a parent or friend, thus sparring with a tadpole before tackling the dragon. For nervous high schoolers facing standardized tests for college admissions, practice is available in the form of review books, review courses, and/or computer quizzes.

Relaxation techniques can also help the anxious student. Three effective strategies for relaxation are mentioned in Michael Bloomquist's *Skills Training for Children with Behavior Disorders*. The first is deep breathing (inhaling deeply and exhaling very slowly), which can be practiced using a candle. When the child is exhaling gradually, the candle will flicker but not go out. The second relaxation technique is alternately tightening and relaxing various muscle groups. This can be explained to the child as switching from being a robot to being a rag doll. The third technique utilizes visualization. The student creates a mental picture of a relaxing setting, perhaps imagines himself floating on a raft on a quiet lake. Older children may also benefit from commercial relaxation tapes or meditation.

Strategies for Remembering

Despite the current de-emphasis on rote learning, the ability to retain information still plays a significant role in academic success. Therefore, to the four common student complaints discussed in the preceding chapter, we must add one more: "I can't remember all this stuff." Unfortunately, most classrooms provide little or no instruction in how to remember. Parents, thinking back on their own experiences as students, can help with good suggestions.

Frank is angrily denouncing his history teacher. Tomorrow morning there's a test on matching the fifty-three African countries and their capitals, and Frank can't remember them. Mnemonic devices (memory helpers) to the rescue. Mother looks over the list. "*Lusaka* makes me think of loose socks," she says. "Now how can we attach that capital to its country, Zambia?"

"I know," Frank shouts. "I'll just imagine Zorro in socks with a big Z on them."

"Great! Let's try another one. Dakar is the capital of Senegal," his mother said. "How can we connect those two names?"

Frank thought a minute, then came up with "It's *dark* in here. I can't *see* anything."

"Terrific!" his mother replies. "Only fifty-one countries to go. Why don't you brainstorm on this further by yourself? If you run out of ideas, maybe your friend Bobby will work on it with you."

Acronyms and mental pictures are also great memory aids. To remember the names of the five Great Lakes, think of the word *homes* (for *H*uron, *O*ntario, *M*ichigan, *E*rie, and *S*uperior). To remember that the Spanish word *mesa* means *table*, visualize a messy table. Once introduced to memory devices such as these, children can quickly learn to apply the methods to their own memorizing tasks.

Letters, rhymes, images, colors, sounds, smells, objects, and movements—any of these can be used to help kids remember. What method is best? That depends upon a child's particular learning style. Some kids remember more by writing information. Leslie, a finalist in a spelling bee, "wrote" each word she was given in the air so that she could "see" it. Joanne was an auditory learner, a terrible speller and a great talker. When Joanne studied, she read and recited the new information aloud. Her oral studying technique got her through law school quite successfully. Kinesthetic learners remember best when they can manipulate objects. Parents should encourage kids to practice with different kinds of learning styles and find out what works best for them. In cases where kids continue to have problems remembering academic facts, a learning specialist can usually help.

Drill, drill, drill. Dull, dull, dull. Children don't want to go over and over spelling words, multiplication tables, geographical facts, historical dates, and so on. To make the task more interesting, parents often work with their younger children, testing them on the spelling words or math facts of the day. Some parents turn drills into mini-games. ("Let's see how many correct multiplication answers you can give me in three minutes. Let's see if you can beat yesterday's score of fifteen.") Parental participation in memorizing tasks is fine in the early grades, but by junior high parents should no longer be expected to do this on a regular basis. Children can practice and drill alone or with friends, once some good techniques for doing so have been learned. But even students in the lower grades can be taught to check themselves. For example, basic math facts can be practiced with a calculator as monitor. The student punches in the digits and the function (addition, subtraction, multiplication, etc.), then gives an answer orally, then punches in the equal sign to find out if the computer agrees.

Here's a flash: in this high-tech age the tried-and-true, old-fashioned flash card is still a great teaching tool. The question is on one side, the answer on the back. It can be used to study definitions, dates, types of rocks, state capitals, etc. Just the process of putting the information on the flash cards helps to get it inside the head. During practice sessions, flash cards can be rearranged so that the student can continue drilling just on the ones he missed last time through the stack. This is a memorizing technique that's ideal for decreasing anxiety the night before the big test. Working with flash cards shows students that they actually know something.

Researchers also recommend a technique called *chunking* to help students remember. If students are asked to memorize the names of the countries in the United Nations, it will be easier to do so after grouping them by continent. Chunking helps students remember by grouping similar things together.

"I can't remember all this" may also be the cry of a child dreading tomorrow's essay exam on a science or social science unit. Effective reading strategies can prepare them for the test. One technique for achieving better retention—probably first described by F. B. Robinson (1970) in *Effective Study*— is called *PQRST*. The letters stand for *preview, question, read, state,* and *test*. Here's the recommended procedure: preview by skimming, ask yourself important questions about the material, read to look for answers to your questions, state the answers in your own words (or if you can't, go back and reread) and test yourself at frequent intervals to be sure you're retaining the important points.

A similar method is called *SQ3R*, which stands for *survey, question, read, recite,* and *review*. This technique, described by D. Rowntree (1983) in *Learn How to Study*, emphasizes previewing by reading the chapter headings first and turning them into questions. (Other questions that may be provided 'at the beginning or end of a chapter should also be utilized to check comprehension and retention.) With specific questions in mind, the student is ready to be an alert reader, a reading detective in search of specific information. The third step is a thorough reading including study of the chapter's visual material—graphs, charts, and photos. Fourth comes recitation, repeating what was learned from reading each section. The final step is review, using the questions created from the headings.

Following the procedures these two systems recommend is, of course, more time-consuming than passive reading. But students need to learn that there are different ways to read to accomplish different goals. Reading a textbook means studying for retention. It is not just a matter of running one's eyes over the page and catching what one can.

It's easier to remember facts when they are meaningful and when they are viewed as part of a pattern. Therefore, to help your child retain information more easily, place it within a context or relate it to other facts the child already knows.

Sometimes parents hear just the opposite of "I can't remember all this." The student says, "I already know how to divide fractions. Why do I have to do more of these problems?" Experts on memory tell us that even after something has been learned, more practice (resulting in what is called *overlearning*) makes the memory stronger. Overlearning increases long-term retention and may also decrease test anxiety.

Test Checklists for Kids

To help your child decrease test anxiety and increase test scores, you might want to photocopy the following suggestions and discuss them with your child.

Test Preparation Techniques

✐ Ask your teacher specific questions about the test. (Will it be objective or essay? Will it be matching or multiple-choice?

Exactly what material will it cover?) That information will help you determine how to study for it.

✎ Predict how you expect to do on the test. Then think of ways that you can improve the prediction. What study techniques might help you do better? Incorporate them into your study plan.

✎ Don't be a study binger. Don't plan a late-night or all-night study session the evening before the big test. Bingeing brings you to the exam exhausted. Last-minute studying doesn't allow time to think about and practice what you've learned.

✎ Make a study plan. Spread out the studying over several days, working on a reasonable segment of the material each day. Leave the day before the test for final reviewing of everything.

✎ Review corrected homework and past quizzes.

✎ Review class notes and textbook questions (with a study buddy, if possible). Look for your past mistakes, and try to correct them.

✎ Try to predict what the test questions might be. Make a list of possible questions, and ask your study buddy to do the same. Then test out your test questions on each other (in person, on the phone, or via E-mail).

✎ Study actively. Don't just reread material. Talk aloud to yourself, explain the material to someone else, or write down answers to questions you think might be asked.

✎ Try not to let test anxiety interfere with your performance. Don't be your own worst enemy. Get a good night's sleep before the test. Be optimistic. Remind yourself that you studied, and that you know enough to do reasonably well.

Remind yourself that one test does not seal your fate forever. Ask yourself, "What's the worst thing that could happen to me if I fail this test?" Chances are, nothing catastrophic.

✐ Study enough! The best medicine for test anxiety is the knowledge that you're well-prepared.

Test-Taking Tips

For objective tests:

✐ Read the directions carefully, and read each item carefully.

✐ Answer what you know first. (You want to get to the end of the test and get credit for everything you know.) Then go back and mull over the questions you're unsure about. But don't spend a lot of time on any one item.

✐ On a multiple choice test with a reading passage, read the choices (possible answers) before you read the passage. Then you know what information you're looking for in the reading.

✐ Be sure you understand how the test is being graded. Is there a greater penalty for a wrong answer than for no answer? In that case don't guess unless you can narrow the possible right answers down to two choices. On the other hand, if no answer will be graded as a wrong answer, it pays to guess on every test item you don't know. *Dr. Sylvia Rimm's Smart Parenting* offers these tips on guessing strategies when you haven't any idea which of several choices is correct:
1. If one answer is much longer than the other, choose that one.
2. If two choices are opposites, choose one of them.
3. If you have no idea what the answer is, choose C. (Teachers like to "bury" correct answers in the middle of the

choices. Anyway, you're more likely to hit some right answers if your guesses are all the same letter.)

- On a multiple choice or true-false test, remember that words such as *always*, *every*, and *only* are more likely to be in a wrong answer. On the other hand, words like *usually* and *sometimes* are more likely to be in correct answers.

- Don't get too creative or offbeat in your thinking. The more obvious interpretation of a test item is likely to be the correct one. Go along with reasonable assumptions of the test writer. Don't be like Willie, who couldn't answer a test question that assumed that Room 1706 was directly below Room 1806 because he knew of a building in which that was not the case.

- Beware of tricks. For example, double negatives can be tricky. Another trick of test writers: one of the choices contains correct information, but it is not the information the question asked for. Example: If a math question asks how much a buyer *paid* for an item that was 25 percent off, don't mark the answer that tells how much the buyer *saved*.

For essay tests:

- Ask beforehand how the test is going to be graded. Will you be graded on writing style, sentence structure, and organization, or is the content all that is being evaluated? Don't spend much time on the quality of the writing if that isn't what's being tested. Instead, be sure you have covered all the points that should be in your answer.

- Before you begin to write, jot down (on scratch paper) the main ideas you want to cover and determine a logical order for presenting them.

✐ Leave yourself time to go back and read what you wrote. Sometimes careless errors creep in; test-takers have even been known to write the *opposite* of what they intended to say. Also, if your writing style is being evaluated, you'll need time to edit and to check mechanics.

✐ Be timewise. If you have several essay questions of equal point value to answer, it's a good idea to divide your time approximately equally among them. However, you may be able to write more quickly about the material you know best.

✐ Answer what you know (or consider easier) first. That will give you confidence and a better idea of how much time you have for the "toughies."

For any test:

✐ Pay attention to time. Note how many questions there are, and estimate how much time you should spend on each question or section.

✐ Mark questions you skipped with a check and any that you guessed at with a question mark. If time allows, go back and reconsider these.

✐ If your teacher says it's okay, before you read the test, write out some of the information you expect to need—formulas, dates, names, etc. Then you don't have to worry that test anxiety will scare away what you studied and actually know.

After the Test

✐ Don't throw a bad test in the wastebasket. Analyze it. Figure out why you got a low grade. Did you make careless mistakes? Did you study the wrong material? Did you spend too much time answering one question? If you can figure out where you went wrong on this test, you'll do better next time. If you can't figure out what you did wrong, ask your teacher (or a parent) to help you.

✎ Keep all your tests and quizzes in folders (one for each subject). They're handy for reviewing for final examinations.

8

Speaking, Not Sparring, with Your Child's Teacher

The Routine Parent-Teacher Conference

"If you were a perfect parent, you'd be a terrible parent," a social worker once told a group of mothers. The same statement might be made about teachers. Children need to accept the fact that even adults who care about them will not always treat them ideally. Parents sometimes lose their temper, forget their promises, or get so preoccupied that they temporarily ignore their children. Even very good teachers occasionally give bad assignments, get angry and say something unkind, get careless and make mistakes, get rushed and explain things poorly. Parents and teachers need to be tolerant of each other's errors and perspectives. Parent-teacher conferences provide excellent opportunities for airing concerns affecting a student's learning.

Most schools provide at least two kinds of opportunities for parent-teacher encounters. One typical event is Parent Night (usually early in the school year), when the teachers speak to groups of parents about the curriculum and academic goals. This is an important meeting to attend. Parents need to know what a child is supposed to master in a given year in order to support those goals and provide appropriate, related enrichment activities. However, these general meetings are not the time to talk to a teacher about the needs of an individual child. In the lower grades private parent-teacher conferences are generally set up for this purpose. In middle school or junior high, when students have different teachers for different subjects, parents may meet with the team of teachers working with their child. Parents of junior high or high school students should also feel free to ask for a conference whenever they are concerned about their child's achievement in a particular subject or course.

Before the Conference

Perhaps the best parental preparation for a parent-teacher conference is to talk to your child about the upcoming event. Ask your child these questions:

- "What activities have you especially enjoyed in this class?" (The answer will give you some positive feedback to give to the teacher.)
- "What would you like me to ask your teacher about?" (This will help you pinpoint areas of confusion or concern.)
- "What good things do you think your teacher is going to tell me about you? Do you think she's going to suggest improvement in any areas?" (This will enable you to determine, after the conference, whether or not your child has a realistic idea about how she is doing and how she is perceived by the teacher.)

In preparation for the conference, it's also a good idea to make some notes about what you want to tell and ask the teacher. It's easy to forget what you wanted to cover once you get into a conference and get distracted by the teacher's comments or hassled by time constraints.

Finally, try to think of something complimentary to say about what has gone on in the classroom thus far. Your comment might reflect your child's enthusiasm about a particular activity: "Mary Ellen just loved the folk tales unit." Or it might reflect your own observations about your child's academic growth: "I think Sam's spelling has improved a lot this year." When talking to teachers, parents tend to focus upon what's bothering them and say too little about successes. Think ahead about a way to say "thank you" in the form of positive feedback.

At the Conference: Topics to Cover

Allow the teacher to direct the course of the conversation, inserting your questions and comments only when they directly relate to the teacher's remarks. Your other questions and explanations should be saved until the teacher has finished his presentation. Before concluding the conference, be sure that the following topics have been covered:

- any major changes in your child's life (health problems, a divorce in the family, etc.)
- the child's behavior at school (Is your child responsible, attentive, cooperative, respectful, and sociable at school?)
- how your child is doing academically, which should answer these questions:

  1. Has she made academic progress since the last conference (or since the beginning of the school year)?
  2. How is she doing academically compared with the class group?
  3. Is she doing all the assigned work, and does the work show effort and understanding?
  4. Is there any academic subject in which she needs additional help or practice?
  5. What do her recent standardized test scores reveal? How do they compare to the previous year's scores? Is there a great discrepancy between her IQ score and her achievement scores? (This could indicate a learning disability.)

When your allotted conference time is up, leave. Other parents are probably waiting. If there's more to discuss about your child, ask for another appointment.

When the Teacher Requests Change

At some parent-teacher conferences, the teacher indicates complete satisfaction with a student's progress and behavior. But don't be too disappointed if that's not your experience. Look at it this way: every good teacher wants every child in her classroom to change. Who wants to see a child go out in June the same as he was in September? Teachers often tell parents things they don't want to hear—that their child is too sloppy, too lazy, too disruptive, and so on. When change is desired, here are appropriate responses:

- *Do* consider having another parent-teacher conference *with the child present.* (In some schools, conferences routinely include the child.) This should not be for the purpose of having an adult on either side bombarding Stephanie with her flaws. Rather, it should be to get *her* perspective on what might lead to improvement.
- *Do* consider a contract. It will probably be between the parent and child, with the teacher providing input as to progress. (See Chapter 4 for specifics.)
- *Do* ask about student mentoring. Schools with mentoring programs have found that they can result in long-term benefits. Children learn well within a social context. Collaborative learning that links a more experienced learner with a novice has been highly successful. Children having academic difficulties usually respond well to assistance from another child in the same grade or from an older student. The equally shiny other side of the mentoring coin is this: the mentor also reaps great benefits. Being a mentor helps to make a child feel valuable. He discovers that he too has something important to contribute. Even at-risk students (who are not very successful in their own grades) can be good teachers of younger chil-

dren. And the mentoring experience can help these students develop more positive attitudes toward school and learning.

- *Do* make a plan. Sometimes teachers complain about a child's behavior but offer no suggestions for bringing about change. The parent may have no idea either. If the parent, child, and teacher cannot agree upon a plan, consult another school professional (for example, a social worker or school psychologist) for advice.
- *Do* ask for teaching tips. If there's an academic weakness and you fear your child will not want to keep practicing "the same old stuff," ask the teacher for suggestions for reviewing in a more interesting way. (Example: Penmanship doesn't always have to be practiced with a paper and pencil. Letters can be written in sand, dirt, even chocolate pudding!)
- *Do* make arrangements for follow-up. Schedule further communication (by phone or note), and be sure the child understands that this will occur. Follow-up should be in the near future (in a week or two) and should continue for at least a few months.
- *Do* talk to your child about the teacher's suggestions and indicate your support of them.
- *Do* encourage your child to make the changes the teacher requests even if you (and/or your child) feel that they aren't significant. It's important for students to get the idea that, where academic work is concerned, the teacher, not the parent, is the ultimate authority.

When a teacher indicates that your child needs to improve in certain areas, avoid these all-too-common reactions:

- *Don't* try to shift the blame onto the teacher, the child's friends, or even yourself: "He wasn't a trouble-maker last year in Mrs. Barrett's class." (It's the teacher's fault.); "It's this new group of friends he has. They're so wild." (The other kids are to blame.); or "I'm no good at math, either." (It's my fault; he has bad math genes.)
- *Don't* pooh-pooh the criticism as coming from a rigid teacher

who doesn't understand that children are just children. Remember that the teacher knows very well how most kids your child's age behave and what they can do. If the teacher tells you that your child needs to improve in a certain area, the suggestion should be taken seriously.

- *Don't* expect or try to bring about change in several areas at once. Work on one problem at a time (probably the most debilitating one first), and realize that improvement will be gradual.
- *Don't* discuss the academic achievements or problems of your other children unless you firmly believe the information will help the teacher better understand the child that is in her class now.
- *Don't* compare and contrast your child to other students in the class. It is not appropriate or helpful for you to discuss them, and it is not ethical for the teacher to do so.
- *Don't* threaten your child with retention or punishment because of school problems. Be optimistic about the child's ability to improve and succeed.

Note: Parents frequently complain that teachers wait too long into the school year before telling them about difficulties their children are having. However, teachers are reluctant to make hasty judgments. They like to wait until they're sure there's a pattern of academic or behavioral difficulty before contacting a parent. One way that parents can encourage quicker reporting of problems is by contacting the teacher at the beginning of the school year, telling the teacher about a difficulty the child has had in the past, and inviting the teacher to call immediately if it recurs. This is not "tattling" on your child. This is intelligent cooperation between adults in order to correct conditions detrimental to learning.

When Homework Is an Issue

Homework issues are high on the list of parent-teacher conference topics. Parents may be too quick to assume that because teachers are the source of the homework they are also the source of the problem. Maybe so, but maybe not. The problem may be the student's. Let's consider the possibilities with what we'll call "the five too's" of homework complaints.

It's too much. Maybe the teacher is assigning too much, or maybe your child is doing more work than was intended. You need to tell the teacher which assignments took your child two weeks longer than forever and find out why.

It's too hard. Did the teacher explain it inadequately, or does your child lack the skills or knowledge needed to do the assignment as expeditiously as the other students? Parents are especially annoyed by homework they themselves cannot do. It's inappropriate to go into a parent-teacher conference expecting the teacher to give you a lesson in sixth grade math or geography. But there's nothing wrong with asking for advice: "Matilda didn't know how to do the last two math assignments. What do you think is the reason for that? What can we do about it? Where can she get help?"

It's too dull. Maybe the teacher is assigning too much of the same thing. But perhaps Dave would find the work less tedious if he would give it his complete attention and get it done promptly instead of prolonging it over a zillion TV commercials. To encourage teachers to give more interesting homework assignments, parents should remember to mention those tasks that their kids seemed to especially enjoy and/or benefit from. Teachers also need to be told that a particular assignment was especially uninteresting. Hearing that in several conferences will make the point clear.

There's too little homework. Kids won't complain about this, but parents sometimes do. Before assuming that the teacher is lazy and not doing her job, consider these possibilities: (1) Your child is doing the work in a perfunctory way, not giving it the time intended; or (2) Your child is a very good student who can do the work quickly. If standardized test scores show that your child's academic skills and knowledge are beyond grade level and continuing to grow, then why worry? Also remember that in the primary grades homework is usually limited to thirty minutes (or less) per day. Stretching the mind is good, but educators believe that kids need time to stretch their legs too.

It's too easy. Don't be too quick to criticize the teacher when your child complains about having to practice what he already knows. Material that is overlearned is retained longer. Practice reinforces and builds confidence. Also, quick and easy homework leaves valuable free time for family enrichment activities. (See Chapters 9, 10, 11, and 12.)

Of greater concern than the quality of the homework is whether or not the child is doing it consistently and adequately. Parents should not be enablers of their children's homework avoidance. Whatever the excuse—"It's stupid work." "I already know that." "The teacher won't even look at it." "I have better things to do with my time." "There's no point in learning this junk."—parents should not support it. It is important to have faith in the teacher's judgment. If it's assigned, assume it's worth doing and insist that your child do it. If parents do not support homework completion, teachers become discouraged and assign less, which means that kids lose out.

If a child is doing the homework correctly (and independently), then test grades in that subject should also be adequate. If they aren't, then parent and teacher need to figure out why not. Are the tests going beyond what's being practiced? Is the child forgetting to review before tests?

Another important question: is the homework being returned to the student with some feedback such as a grade, praise of what's good, clear indications of what's wrong, and suggestions for improvement? Does the student look at the corrected work and understand the comments? If children are having academic difficulty, parents may want to work out a plan for seeing that corrected homework arrives home and gets discussed with the student.

Believe it or not, these days there are two i's in the word *homework*. The first one stands for *individualization*. Individualized assignments are usually popular with parents because they are designed to meet the interests or needs of specific students. Individualized assignments may be worked out at parent-teacher conferences or given directly to students who demonstrate a need for additional practice with a certain skill or certain academic content. Individualized assignments are also a way to provide challenging work for students at the top of the class. Assignments are also individualized when students are given some choice about the homework they do. Teachers sometimes encourage their students to decide for themselves what skills they need more practice with. Homework also becomes individualized when a child has some choice (for example, in selecting a book to read or a project to do). Parents can suggest individualization and choice in homework assignments and give teachers positive feedback when their children respond well to these options. However, parents and students must realize that teachers don't have the time to individualize every assignment.

The second i stands for *interactive homework*. This trend has become significant enough to earn a write-up in the *Wall Street Journal* (June 6, 1997). The article describes interactive homework as "families studying together: playing math games, keeping weather charts, recording the phases of the moon, researching tidal waves on the Internet." Some parents think it's great. Others are freaked out by the burden it places upon their time (especially if they have three or four children). Sometimes parents are embarrassed when they can't participate because they don't possess the necessary skills or knowledge. When assigning interactive assignments, teachers need to think about the abilities and possible limitations of the parents in their community.

Interactive homework can begin as early as kindergarten. One kindergarten teacher described this interactive assignment she gave as "homewalk homework." The child and parent take a walk together, taking care to notice interesting things along the way. Then the child dictates to the parent the highlights of the excursion, and the parent writes up the child's adventure, which is read aloud in class the following week.

For interactive homework at its best, educators need look no further than a federally funded project called Teachers Involve Parents in Schoolwork (TIPS), developed by Johns Hopkins University's Center on School, Family, and Community Partnerships. According to codirector Joyce L. Epstein, "Research shows that parent involvement improves student achievement, attitudes, homework, report card grades, and aspirations. Surveys of parents show that most families want to be able to talk with, monitor, encourage, and guide their children as students, but they say they need more information from the schools about how to help their children at home." To meet this need, the Center has developed TIPS prototype interactive activities for various grade levels in math, language arts, science, and health. TIPS also provides tips for teachers who want to write their own interactive homework corresponding specifically to their own classroom instruction.

TIPS assignments require a child to talk to someone at home about what he is learning in class. Example: one language arts activity asks the student to look around the kitchen and find examples of phrases with nouns and adjectives, such as *crunchy cookies* or *soapy water*. The child writes his list, and then the adult adds an adjective to each of the child's phrases. Then parent and child talk about categories of nouns found in the kitchen, such as fruits, vegetables, or utensils. TIPS lessons such as this encourage parents to participate with children in discussing, applying, and extending what was learned in class. The teaching remains the teacher's responsibility; the homework remains the child's responsibility; the parent's role is intended, defined, and limited so that the parent shares in but does not dominate the discovery of knowledge. TIPS assignments also ask for feedback from the adult participant, indicating if the student seemed to understand and enjoy the activity. Teachers can then revise and improve lessons based upon these comments. Thus, TIPS assignments complete the circle—providing feedback from school to home and from home to school. Parents can encourage schools to get involved with TIPS by providing teachers and administrators with explanatory materials. For more information about TIPS, contact The Center on School, Family, and Community Partnerships, The Johns Hopkins University, 3505 North Charles Street, Baltimore, MD 21218.

Obviously, not all of a child's homework should be interactive. However, we see the use of some interesting, student-dominated interactive homework as highly beneficial for many reasons. Interactive homework gets the family focused upon what's being studied in school. It provides a chance for the student to "show off" what he's learned. It also provides an opportunity for one-on-one instruction, which is limited at school. The parent can assess the child's comprehension, clarify misconceptions, and communicate with the teacher about what confused the student. When asked "What did you learn in school today?" some kids take the Fifth Amendment. Interactive homework provides a way for adults to open and develop a dialogue about school lessons.

It's not always easy to arrange time for interactive homework—especially when both parents work, when there's only one adult in the household, or when kids have a hectic extracurricular schedule. It's helpful if interactive homework always comes home the same day of the week and is not due the next day. It's also a good idea for schools to explain the concept of interactive homework to parents before sending home these kinds of assignments. Finally, schools should print interactive activities on a specially designated colored paper so that they are not overlooked by parents.

When Parents Worry: Stress, Grades, Retention, and Values

Many parents are concerned because their children find school stressful. Some parents think that children's lives should be free from anxiety, problems, and the embarrassment of making mistakes. (Adults sometimes forget how much they learned and benefited from their own past mistakes.) They want their children's lives to be easy, stress-free, and full of fun, fun, fun. Teachers, on the other hand, tend to focus upon challenges that will lead to growth. Teachers wants kids to learn that achievement and praise come from hard work. How much stress is too much? When does challenge become frustration? Parents and teachers often disagree about where the line should be drawn. Many parents want their kids to come home smiling because the teacher said everything the child did was wonderful. Teachers want to be stingier with praise so that it has more value. Empty praise doesn't have much weight. School gives every child some struggles, worries, and hard times. That's to be expected, and it is often beneficial.

Grades are another area of parental concern. Laura, receiving her essay back with a C+ on it, was disappointed and defensive. "My father thought it was a good paper," she told the teacher. Children need to understand that where grades are concerned the teacher's word is law. At a parent-teacher conference it's pointless to argue about whether a grade was fair or not. Rather, if grades are low, the parent should ask what can be done to improve them. However, if a teacher is giving a child lower grades because of his or her behavior, this is a matter to discuss with the principal.

An especially painful parental worry: retention (once called "flunking"). Research and experience have convinced us that children who have been retained do little or no better than weak students who were not retained. In general, retention seems a bad idea. However, it seems to do least psychological damage when the grade being repeated is kindergarten or first grade or when a child is changing schools. Occasionally, it helps a child who is hopelessly behind get back into the ball game. In recent years, in more and more states, retention is no longer a decision made by parents and educators after considering the total child. Instead, it is objectively dictated by standardized test scores. Today's more stringent promotion policies put greater pressure upon parents and teachers to help kids keep up in school.

Parental concerns sometimes focus not upon their own children's academic accomplishments but upon the school system in general. (That's why about 1.3 million American kids are home-schooled.) Parental complaints may range from "The school doesn't teach enough" to "The school pushes kids too hard." Some parents don't approve of what the school is teaching or how the school is teaching. Should school instruction focus upon the transmission of a body of knowledge, or should the emphasis be upon thinking skills? Parents may feel that their neighborhood school is emphasizing one of these and inadequately teaching the other. Should schools be teaching values, and if so, what if the school's values are not the parents'? (Example: An organization called "Facing History in Ourselves" creates curriculum to help students overcome racial and religious prejudice. Students exposed to these ideas may bring home attitudes vastly different from their parents'.)

A parent-teacher conference is neither the time nor place to debate the strengths and weaknesses of the school's curriculum, pedagogical approach, or values. Parents with general concerns in those areas can become active in the PTA, run for the school board or council, or become involved in school policy-making in other ways. The purpose of the parent-teacher conference is to discuss the specifics of a particular child's school life.

When a Child Is Unhappy at School

Sometimes parental concerns expressed at conferences are based upon what the child has complained about, and the child's complaint may or may not be justified. "My daughter feels you don't know she's alive," one mother reported to the teacher. The parent did not accuse the teacher of ignoring her daughter. She simply indicated that the child saw things that way. And the teacher realized that because Juanita was quiet and hard-working, no problem in any way, she hadn't been receiving her share of attention.

Marlene came home crying after her teacher had said to her, "I know a two-year-old whose scribbling looks better than your writing." Marlene told her mother, "It's not Mrs. Robbin's job to make me feel bad." Right on! When teachers forget the powerful impact their words can have on kids, sometimes parents have to remind them.

"My teacher hates me," ten-year-old Felicia told her mother. "She never lets me be messenger. She says my science notebook is too messy. She hates me, and I hate her. I'm never going back to school again!"

Many parents of school-aged children have, at one time or another, heard a similar tale. "Should I interfere or not interfere?" parents in these situations ask themselves. "Will the teacher resent it if I complain? If I don't complain, won't my child just go on suffering?"

Parents are right to hope for a mutually respectful teacher-student relationship. Students who consider their school progress important and attainable will probably continue to pay attention in class and do assigned work even if they don't like the teacher. But for students who are ambivalent about schoolwork, who question its value and their own abilities, a good relationship with the teacher can make a huge difference.

"My teacher is mean," "My teacher doesn't like me"—statements such as these, whether true or false, merit parental attention. But of what sort? Before blaming the teacher, a parent should consider four pertinent questions: Have the child's past relationships with other teachers or figures of authority been stressful? With such people, has the youngster run into problems similar to the one he now faces at school? Do his expectations of school life seem unrealistic? Could he have some reason for creating or inventing difficulties at school?

In the following situations, the school problem has originated with the youngster.

The Attention Grabber

Ted's chief complaint was that he rarely got the special privileges enjoyed by classmates. ("Jimmy's been hall monitor three times already! I've only been picked once.") Ted's mother was concerned enough to pay a visit to the school psychologist, who knew the family well. She helped the mother understand Ted's desire to be singled out by the adults in his world. With his older brother away at school, Ted was the center of attention at home and expected the same spot in the limelight at school. In the classroom, therefore, he felt rejected when his teacher treated him like all the other children.

Ted badly needed lessons in the sharing of adult regard. On family outings, the psychologist felt, he should be encouraged to invite a friend so that he would gain practice in sharing parental attention. In school he needed to understand that the teacher's attention has to be shared by some twenty-five kids and that extra attention is often given to another student not because the teacher likes him better but because that child needs help more.

Bright and ambitious children, only children, children who have routinely been teacher's pet in the past—all may share Ted's problem. An insistent mother might have talked Ted's teacher into giving him more privileges. But catering to a child's wishes does not help him to get along in a group. And learning to work successfully with others is one of the most valuable lessons derived from school.

The "Neglected" Child

Marilyn's problem may sound similar to Ted's, but the cause and the solution were quite different. After just three days in kindergarten, Marilyn came home complaining that her teacher never gave her the good crayons. Her parents nodded wearily. The second child in a family of three girls, Marilyn often assumed the role of Cinderella at home too. "Janet's Christmas present is nicer than mine," she would sulk. "Nancy got more candy than I did." Marilyn's parents had been shrugging off complaints of this sort for some time. But now that she was starting school, it seemed appropriate to discuss Marilyn's feelings of resentment with the teacher. "I know this isn't your fault," the mother began, "but Marilyn feels cheated by life in general, so naturally she feels cheated in school too. Can you suggest any way in which we can both help her?" The teacher was sympathetic and offered to make doubly sure that Marilyn didn't get slighted.

Not all those who feel neglected at home react to school the way Marilyn did. Some try to bribe or charm their teachers into providing the mothering they want. Five-year-old Paula, for example, clung to her teacher's side all day long. She asked to have her hair combed, her ribbons tied; several times a day she would hug the teacher and whisper, "I love you." These attempts to establish an intimate relationship with the teacher are usually doomed to disappointment and thus only help to confirm the child's sense of being unloved and unlovable. Parents of children like Marilyn and Paula should make a special effort to spend time with them that doesn't include the other children—an occasional shopping trip just with Mommy or a Saturday lunch alone with Daddy. Such attention can make the insecure child feel less like a waif.

An older child who complains of being ignored in class can often benefit from a frank talk with a parent. "Mrs. Gordon never calls on me during current events," sixth-grader Jeremy grumbled.

"Do you have something important to say?" his father asked. "If you want to be called on often, be sure that when you raise your hand you have something worthwhile to contribute, something that hasn't been said before."

Another sixth grader protested, "I never get to do the good jobs, like feeding the fish or decorating the bulletin board."

"When you've had special jobs before, have you remembered to do them?" her mother asked. "Have you shown that you can handle extra responsibility?" Parents can and should help kids learn this important principle—by altering their own behavior, children can usually get others to treat them the way they want to be treated.

The "Baby"

This child wants to have everything done for him and little expected of him. In school he wants more help than the teacher feels he needs. Five-year-old Barry knows that by pretending he can't button his jacket or put on his boots he can get extra attention from adults. Ten-year-old Jeffrey knows that if he acts more uncertain than he really is about handling fractions, his teacher will come over and check his work.

When a child is able to get along on his own, however, he should not have an adult constantly hovering over him. "She won't help me," the dependent child may complain about his teacher. "She doesn't like me." But no one finds an ersatz baby attractive. The teacher may be trying to help him grow up. The parent should help too by not doing tasks for a child that he is capable of doing for himself.

The Struggler

"I worked on that theme for five hours," moaned Kevin, "and my English teacher only gave me a C." Among the saddest complaints that a parent hears are the ones that come from the bewildered, bleary-eyed struggler. Hard work doesn't always bring top grades. If a conscientious child lacks the academic skills to be an A student, hours and hours of studying are unlikely to produce an A for him.

If the struggler feels that his parents will be disappointed by less than A work, he will probably consider himself a failure—and be unhappy. The child who has a need to be outstanding but cannot satisfy this need in school should be helped to find other areas where he can excel: sports, a hobby, community work, scouting, and so on. Both the child and his parents should learn to derive satisfaction from what the youngster can do well. Parents should be pleased when their child has the interest and the perseverance to do his very best in school—even if the result is only average.

The "Martyr"

Aaron describes himself as the totally innocent victim of a cruel and unjust teacher: "I get blamed for everything. *Mark* starts a fight, but she sends *me* to the principal's office." A child who consistently plays the martyr is probably doing so to gain attention both at school and at home. If he cannot find circumstances to be the victim of, he may create trouble by purposely annoying his teacher or classmates. The "martyr" may not realize that his own behavior is the source of his problem. But the fact that a child consistently presents himself as an innocent victim is cause for investigation.

The mother of a child like this can begin by asking, "What makes you think your teacher is always picking on you?" Then, by analyzing the situation as he presents it, she can try to help him see his part in creating school difficulties. Before ending such a discussion, the mother should indicate that she will not interfere at school because she doesn't think he is being victimized. If a youngster learns that his complaints do not win him instant partisanship at home, his behavior at school is likely to improve.

Whenever parents feel, after a fair examination, that the problem is chiefly the child's, they should try to handle it at home. If, however, they conclude that the child's complaints are justified and that he is being treated unfairly, then a parent-teacher conference is certainly in order. It is natural for parents to feel anger toward a teacher who has made their child unhappy. Even so, to accomplish their goal—the alteration of the teacher's behavior—they should keep in mind that little will be gained by angry accusations. The teacher who has hurt a child's feelings has probably done so not out of hostility, but through inexperience, oversight, or poor judgment.

Many teachers want to be considered strict, but almost no one wants a reputation for being mean. Eager to have students learn, inexperienced teachers may assign work that is too difficult for some students and then scold them for not doing well. New teachers may not recognize typical behavior for a particular age level and view normal restlessness and curiosity as a threat to their authority. Teachers afraid of losing control can get unreasonably angry with a child who cracks a joke and temporarily interrupts a lesson. However, when the teacher is well-intentioned and wants to help children, tactful parents can work things out.

But let's face it: among all the teachers who deserve apples, there are a few bad apples, twisted teachers who enjoy humiliating students. (Example: a bizarre news story told of a teacher who punished a student for not doing homework by tying him to his desk and urging his classmates to pinch him!) Some teachers involve themselves in an ongoing battle against "troublemakers"—taking every opportunity to send them to the principal or report misdeeds to their parents, deprive them of school activities they especially enjoy, or belittle and embarrass them in front of classmates. If your child's school life is being made miserable by an unduly harsh teacher, you should certainly interfere. But the intervention should be based upon convincing evidence. No one's reputation and career should be put at stake lightly.

When you come to talk to the teacher who is causing your child unhappiness, start by assuming that the teacher is a well-intentioned person who has, perhaps, made a mistake. Accusations will probably be denied, so avoid them. Instead, demonstrate confidence in the teacher's concern with a comment such as this: "I felt sure you'd want to know that Linda was very upset when she came home from school last Friday." When you tell her why Linda was upset, use the child's own words. Also mention any behavior that shows how the incident affected your child, for example, difficulty falling asleep, loss of appetite, fear of going to school, or faking illness in order to stay home from school.

Nothing is gained by trying to intimidate the teacher. A teacher who feels that her behavior was in the best interest of the student won't be cowed by your threat to go to the principal. If the teacher is willing to cooperate and work out a plan to improve the student-teacher relationship, there is no need to involve the principal. If the teacher is unwilling to make any changes and the existing situation is unacceptable to you, then don't bother threatening to tell the principal. Just do it.

If, as a last resort, the principal is consulted, should you request a room transfer? This decision can be made only after a careful analysis of the personalities involved. In general it is better for both child and teacher to learn to get along. But sometimes teacher and student are such opposites (for example, a creative, sloppy, casual kid and an extremely compulsive, rigid teacher) that it's difficult for them to work together productively. In an extreme situation the child should be given a fresh start. If the teacher sees only negatives and nothing good in your child, then change is for the best.

When student-teacher conflicts are worked out successfully—and most can be—they provide a valuable lesson in human relations. No matter who was at fault, your child should get this message: people who want to be liked must learn to be likeable.

9

Providing Enriching Experiences

Enrichment: What Is It?

A tow-headed Mormon boy wearing a large straw hat was seated beside his father, who was driving a horse-drawn wagon near the front of a lengthy wagon train. The year? 1997. This family was participating in a sesquicentennial celebration, a reenactment of their ancestors' 1846–47 cross-country (1,300-mile) trek from Illinois to Utah. The boy was learning history by reliving it. This experience is a fine example of enrichment.

Effective enrichment gives students experiences that make learning more accessible and desirable to them. Enrichment can help kids discover how to learn, why it's important to learn, and what they want to learn. Most parents strive to give their children enriching experiences; some are more successful at it than others. Before delving into enrichment strategies and materials, parents should heed these wise words of Ralph Waldo Emerson: "Nothing great was ever achieved without enthusiasm." From the many possible forms of enrichment you can introduce to your children, choose those you genuinely enjoy. Take your child to a science museum if you have a real interest in what's there or really want to learn more about science. If not, don't go. If you're bored on the excursion, you'll probably teach your child that science is boring. Whether you like it or not, as parents you teach who you are. However, parents can learn and grow, too.

Parents can help their children become more successful students by offering experiences that use academic skills, expand knowledge, arouse intellectual curiosity, and encourage learning goals. Enrichment doesn't require a lot of information, talent, or money. Time is what's needed—time spent sharing knowledge and learning new things along with children.

General Enrichment Tips

To create an enriching home environment, here are some simple but important things parents can do.

Have real conversations with your children.

Talk to your child as you would to a friend. By that, we mean try to make interesting conversation, sharing stories about the experiences that made your day an event. Dinner-table talk should steer clear of scolding and teachy-preachy lectures. Instead, discuss what happened to you that day that was funny, annoying, exciting, surprising, or scary. Ask your kids about those same kinds of happenings. Discuss current events and share opinions about the news. Parents who are passionate about public issues teach their children values and concern for the outside world. When you and your children watch TV together, take the time to share reactions to what was viewed. Family conversation should also include occasional discussion of children's goals and how education relates to the achievement of these goals. Family "business"—who should do which chores, what rules the household should live by, where the family should go on the next vacation—can be discussed at regularly scheduled (perhaps weekly) family meetings. Meetings such as these are ideal for teaching respect for everyone's input as well as the processes of democratic decision-making.

From conversations with adults, kids pick up myriad skills, such as new vocabulary, more complex sentence structure, reasoning strategies, general information, attitudes, and values. Important things also happen when adults listen to kids. Children who are listened to at home gain confidence to initiate conversations with adults outside the home. They will find it easier to ask a teacher or a librarian for help or a policeman for directions. In addition children need opportunities to run their ideas by adults and get adult response to their kids'-eye view of the world.

In too many households everyone is too busy for worthwhile conversation. Writing in *Parade* (August 3, 1997), CBS essayist Bill Bradley says, "On weekdays, working mothers spend an average of 50 minutes a day with their children; working fathers give their children just 12 minutes a day." What about your family? How much time do you and your children spend in real conversation and joint activities? Keep track for a week. You may be surprised at how little time you share. Try to increase it.

Supply advanced organizers.

Good family conversation can supply what educators call *advanced organizers*. An advanced organizer prepares a child for what's coming, focuses thinking, and encourages prediction. Here's an example: As the McDermott family drove toward Hannibal, Missouri (the home town of Mark Twain), Sandra McDermott told her three children about her favorite parts of *Tom Sawyer* and read some sections of the novel aloud. Then they talked about what sites they expected to see in Hannibal: Mark Twain's childhood home, the white picket fence, Tom's cave, the Mississippi River. By the time the family arrived in Hannibal, the children were eager to explore, to see the real places that they had just heard about. Many advanced organizers are much briefer than this example. Advanced organizers give a child's experiences a focus and a personal touch. They help children more closely relate to what they're learning.

Share who you are with your child.

This suggestion involves both talking and doing. Share your occupation with your child by talking about what you do and by taking your child to work. (This activity can benefit boys as well as girls.) Talk about your hobbies, and invite your child to share them with you. We all know these clichés: children follow in their parents' footsteps; the apple doesn't fall far from the tree. Why are these sayings true? Kids respond to their parents' conveyed joy in the activities that constitute their work or recreation. Participating in adult activities helps children to set goals, and these goals provide motivation for working hard to prepare for the future.

Share stories about your family and ethnic heritage. These help to give children a sense of identity. Nowadays cultural diversity is a major theme in schools. All children need to know about their heritage, its customs and values. In school they may be asked to tell or write about it.

Take an interest in your child's interests.

You can have fun, learn something new, and get to know your child better when you take an interest in your child's hobbies and projects. Adults shouldn't move in and take over, but their assistance can help a child accomplish far more than what the youngster could do alone. Scott, for example, wanted to build an electric rock board game. It would display several types of rocks that his class had studied. When a "player" correctly matched each rock to its name, a light would go on. He had the vision but not the know-how. To get Scott started on this project, his mother (who had always considered geology a terrible bore) took him to a rock shop, where, to her surprise, she had a wonderful time helping to select specimens for the board. Scott's father agreed to help with the electrical work involved in constructing the board, although he wasn't especially handy and had to get advice from a friend. With parental help Scott built his game, and it became a popular item in the school library. Family projects that grow out of a child's interests can be enriching for everyone involved. They also help family members build ties and happy memories.

Let your child be your teacher.

Switch roles now and then, and let your child teach you something. It may be a game, a brief dialogue in a foreign language, or a computer skill. You can also become the learner when your child takes you through a museum that she's recently visited on a school trip. Whatever the activity, the process gives you a chance to demonstrate that learning is fun and a life-long process. Your techniques for learning (repeating, reviewing, questioning, practicing, etc.) also help your child discover how a student of anything learns. Your mistakes and struggles with the learning process prove to a child that learning something new is difficult for everybody.

Ask for your child's help.

Sure, it's easier to do it yourself than to coach your child through awkward first attempts. But long-term, it is in the best interests of parents and children to push kids toward greater self-sufficiency. So ask your child for help. (Advance notice is nice. Don't decide you could use Joe's help with the laundry just as he's on his way out for a bike ride.)

All children should have regular household responsibilities. (Let's not call them "chores.") In addition to doing their regularly assigned tasks, kids are usually willing to help (and sometimes even flattered to be asked) when Mom or Dad requests assistance with something the parent is building, cooking, painting, or planting. Children can learn much from working one-on-one with an adult who's enjoying a task and also enjoys teaching the skills involved.

Children can handle many adult tasks with just a little coaching from a parent on the sidelines. Preparing a meal is an excellent enrichment activity. Shopping requires reading labels and handling money. Food preparation requires reading recipes and measuring. Being the chef of the day requires planning, so it hones organizational skills. It may also require problem-solving skills if the recipe calls for margarine, and there isn't any in the house.

Planning a family vacation is another activity that kids can handle with some adult assistance. Kids can write, E-mail, or phone for information about the site. They can consider various modes of transportation and determine the approximate travel time. If it's a car trip, they can check out the best route to drive and serve as navigators. They can estimate the cost of the trip. They can plan the daily activities during the trip. These tasks involve reading, writing, math, geography, and time management considerations. Besides the enrichment factor, there's another possible bonus: when the kids help plan the vacation, they will be more invested in making it enjoyable for everyone, and gripes will be kept to a minimum.

Use enrichment to respond to your child's academic weaknesses.

Whether the weakness is perceived or real, at-home enrichment can be a significant source of help. Children are quick to jump to conclusions such as "I'm no good at math" or "I can't write." Parents can help kids use math or writing skills at home in ways that will give them greater confidence. If the school's approach to the material didn't work, find a new way to help your child develop a particular skill. Fortunately, these days, entertaining academic materials abound. Chapters 10 through 12 offer many specific tips on academic enrichment. The point to be made here is that home enrichment can provide a noncompetitive, slower-paced way to review material that was insufficiently learned in school.

Getting kids to practice their weakest academic areas can be tricky. Roger got a C in math this year. He evidently missed some important concepts or computational skills. These may cause him to fall further behind the next year. Roger's mother buys a book of math games and a computer program for reviewing (with parental help when needed). But her son may balk if (1) he perceives of the review work as punishment for his low grade; or (2) he thinks his parents are forcing this work upon him for their own ego-satisfaction because they want to brag about a son who's an academic whiz-kid. Roger's parents must make it clear that review will help *Roger* by making next year's math class easier and more comfortable for him. He will not be motivated to review for his parents' sake.

Encourage enrichment activities that develop your child's talents and interests.

George is a terrible athlete—slow, uncoordinated, and unwanted on any team. But he no longer feels bad about this. He's joined a drama group and enjoys the camaraderie and performance opportunities provided by this activity. Kids who become good at something gain a sense of self-worth, so it pays to allow a child to become even better at what she already does well. For children with the talent and interest, music or art lessons are great. Also, find out whether your community's zoo, planetarium, or museums of art, history, or science offer weekend classes for kids. These kinds of classes allow children to pursue specific intellectual interests and meet other kids who share their fascinations.

Take your child places.

Every excursion with an adult can be a learning experience for a child if there's good conversation during the activity. As children accompany their parents and help their parents with whatever they're doing, they learn about adult roles and responsibilities and how to handle them. Today in so many families both parents work, and their children are enrolled in day care or after-school programs. Parents and children spend less time together today than they did fifty years ago. That's a fact of contemporary life. But make opportunities to be together whenever you can.

Interact with interactive museum exhibits.

One of the most enriching and exciting parent-child excursions is to a museum where "hands-on" is the rule. These days, most museums have some interactive exhibits. The nation's approximately 200 children's museums emphasize interactive exhibits, which allow kids to "play at learning," in the words of Karen Harrison, past president of the Board of Trustees of the Chicago Children's Museum. These days, every major urban area has a children's museum. In addition to Chicago, other cities with outstanding children's or interactive museums are Indianapolis (home of the largest children's museum), Boston, San José, Minneapolis, Houston, San Francisco, Denver, Memphis, Brooklyn, and Philadelphia. Children's museum exhibits deal with the cultural arts, social sciences, and in some facilities, the sciences. Many of these museums have websites that can be used to provide advanced organizer material prior to a visit and/or extended learning experiences afterward.

Specific wonders inside five major children's museums (in Indianapolis, Jersey City, Chicago, San Francisco, and Boston) are described in the *New York Times* article "From Mazes to Millipedes: 5 Museums for Young Minds" (June 29, 1997). The article calls these institutions "lively, colorful places" with "waterworks, climbing structures, bubble-blowing equipment and gigantic insects," places where "learning is approached with more levity than gravity." In these museums you'll find truly entertaining academic enrichment.

Help your child become a better problem solver.

It's often referred to as *metacognition*. What is it? In his book *Learning Makes Sense*, John Abbott, director of the United Kingdom's Education 2000 Foundation, gives this definition: "The ability to 'think about thinking,' to be consciously aware of yourself as a problem-solver, and to monitor and control one's mental processing." Metacognition has engaged the attention of cognitive scientists since the early 1980s, and it has by now become a concern of teachers and parents too. How can you help your child develop good problem-solving strategies? Here are a few suggestions:

- Don't rush in with ready-made adult solutions to your children's problems. Let your child come up with his or her own list of possible strategies for dealing with a problem. Point out that there's always more than one way to handle a problem.

- Have your child take his list of possible strategies and cross off the ones that he thinks would be least effective.
- Discuss the pros and cons of the remaining strategies.
- Ask your child to select the one that seems best and try it.
- Evaluate later. Did the strategy selected solve the problem? Why or why not?

Problem solving and other thinking skills can be refined by games. Old standbys such as checkers, chess, bridge, Battleship, and Clue are well worth playing, and there are a multitude of new board games and computer games available.

Kids also have to put on their thinking caps to come up with their own endings to unfinished stories. Your local library probably has several of Donald J. Sobol's *Encyclopedia Brown* books. These are short mysteries for the reader to solve, written in a simple style but often challenging enough to require adults to sneak a peek at the answer key. Also very popular are George Shannon's *Stories to Solve* and *More Stories to Solve*. These present folk tales from around the world and ask the reader to figure out how the problem was handled. (The answer—telling "how it was done"—follows each story.) These are wonderful materials for family read-alouds and discussions.

"Dilbert" reprinted by permission of United Features Syndicate, Inc.

Will Enriching Your Child Leave You Poor?

For enriching a child's environment, there are many things you can buy—books, a calculator, a computer, software, educational games, an encyclopedia, and so on. But you don't need to buy everything and spend a fortune. Most libraries have computers for public use and educational software and videos to take out. Libraries also have activity books describing interesting games that can be made from inexpensive materials everyone has in the house. Kids also can borrow or trade to get access to a greater variety of games, books, and software.

One way to save money is to be a good browser. There is so much material available related to child development and academic skills. To find what's best and reasonably priced, you need to look around. For books on enrichment in specific subject areas, look in libraries or bookstores (especially the parenting sections) and visit stores for teachers and parents. (They're commonly listed under "school supplies" in the yellow pages.) Shop for educational games in these teacher-parent stores also, or browse through toy stores or toy manufacturers' catalogs. To find out about educational computer programs, ask in stores such as Comp USA or Best Buy, read computer magazines (such as *Family PC*) for reviews of new software, call the major software manufacturers for catalogs, or check their websites.

Attitudes That Enrich

Parents can teach their kids many things, but in the end the most valuable enrichment parents can offer is the modeling of positive attitudes toward learning. On Mother's Day, 1997, *Parade Magazine* (the Sunday newspaper supplement) ran an inspiring article about this kind of parent. Sonya Carson, at the age of thirteen, "married" a man who neglected to tell her that he already had a wife. A few years and two sons later, Sonya's "husband" deserted her, leaving this poor and poorly educated teenager with two boys to raise by herself. Given this scenario, one might have predicted that the boys would become high-school dropouts. But today one is an engineer and the other a world-renowned surgeon, famous for his technique for separating conjoined twins. (The story of this brilliant African-American's medical achievements is told in his autobiography, *Gifted Hands*.) "My children are everything I hoped they'd be," Sonya told the article's author, Michael Ryan. Indeed, nearly all parents would feel the same way, thrilled to have children who succeeded academically and found meaningful careers as a result.

So how did Sonya Carson do it? "Every mom knows that a child isn't going to hear too much of what she says," Sonya explains. "It's what she does that's important. You have to start living what you say." Sonya provided a household structured for academic work. She required her boys to do their homework and limited their TV viewing to two shows a week. She required them to spend a large chunk of their spare time reading. But, most important, Sonya taught her children to respect knowledge and be willing to struggle for it. How? By doing these things herself. Determined to obtain an education, she reversed the usual parent-child roles and enlisted her boys' help in improving her own reading skills. Eventually, she returned to school, earned her GED, and became an interior decorator. Sonya Carson transmitted her love and respect for education to her boys, thereby motivating them to achieve in school and succeed in their adult lives. That's effective enrichment.

Catalogs for Educational Games, Toys, Books, and Supplies

Constructive Playthings: phone (800) 448-4112;
fax (816) 761-9295
J. L. Hammett Co.: phone (800) 333-4600; fax (800) 873-5700

The Learning Post: phone (800) 562-1192; fax (847) 885-4172

The Learning Tree (Gray's Distributing Co.): phone (800) 688-2959; fax (773) 769-6431

Thinking-Skills Books

For preschool through third grade:

101 Amusing Ways to Develop Your Child's Thinking Skills and Creativity, Sarina Simon. Los Angeles: Lowell House, 1996.

Thinking Games to Play with Your Child, Cheryl Tuttle, M.Ed., and Penny Paquette. Los Angeles: Lowell House, 1997.

For grades two to six:

Ten-Minute Thinking Tie-ins, Murray Suid and Wanda Lincoln. Palo Alto, CA: Monday Morning Books, Inc., 1992.

10

Hunting for Information

School is in session, and the hunt is on! Tracking down elusive facts may bring Dad to the library and Mom to the Internet. But please don't forget the student. As with other homework assistance, research is something parents should do *with* the child, not *for* the child. One of the most valuable forms of enrichment parents can provide is helping children learn how to find information. Many kids become adept investigators by absorbing school instruction, asking librarians for help, and doing computer research with friends. But most can benefit from some parental help in developing fact-finding skills.

Library Research

Don't let anyone tell you that the computer has made the library obsolete. Rather, computer technology has made libraries high-tech. If you haven't been in a library for a while, you'll probably discover that your local library has discarded the card catalog and replaced it with a much more informative computer database. Remember the

Reader's Guide to Periodical Literature? It's still there, but most people looking for information in magazines find the computer databases much quicker and easier to use. Some kids want to stay home and do all their researching on America Online or the Internet. But library reference books often answer questions more quickly and accurately. In Salzman and Pondiscio's *The Ultimate On-line Homework Helper*, the authors describe a research race between groups of students, some using computers and others using library reference books. The library won!

Take your child to the library—early and often. Even a preschooler is not too young to visit and benefit from the library. Get your young child her own library card. Show her where age-appropriate materials are located—books, records, CDs, magazines, and computer software. Introduce her to the children's librarian. Make sure she understands that asking for help is not bothering the librarian, that the librarian's job is to provide assistance to library users. Ask the librarian what special programs the library offers to young children. Some even have storyreading pajama parties!

Kids in the intermediate and upper elementary grades can be motivated to tour the library with Mom or Dad in one of the following situations: (1) The student wants help researching a specific school assignment. (2) The student and parent are going "just for fun." The student has a list of questions (based upon personal interests), and the parent and child are going to look for the answers. (3) The parent offers to participate in a library tour, just to find out where materials are located. A library tour should include input from the parent, child, and reference librarian. The tour should be hands-on, including practice in using a computer to locate a book and using a database to search for magazine articles on a particular topic. Today's high-tech library makes magazine research a breeze. After you find an article you want in the database, it's possible to send an abstract of it (or the entire article if it's on the computer) to your own personal computer (PC) via E-mail. You can then retrieve it and print it out at home.

When giving your child a general library tour, begin by pointing out major sections of the library, indicating where the following types of materials are located: fiction, nonfiction, reference materials, magazines, newspapers, atlases, videos, and computer software. Some handy references that upper elementary school students should be acquainted with are the following:

- an unabridged dictionary
- encyclopedias (*World Book* is excellent for elementary school students.)
- almanacs (such as *Information Please Almanac* or *The Universal Almanac*)
- *Reader's Guide to Periodical Literature* (Note: some major general magazines are not on the computer databases, for example, *National Geographic* and *Consumer's Reports*, so *Reader's Guide* is still useful.)
- *Roget's 21st Century Thesaurus* (1992) (This dictionary style version is easier to use than the original Roget's, which is organized by topic.)
- Bartlett's *Familiar Quotations*
- *The Guinness Book of Records* (Everyone finds this expert on excesses fascinating. A pumpkin weighing 827 pounds, a bird with a 1,728-word vocabulary, a six-year-old college student, a wedding dress that cost $7 million—kids love it!)

With an upcoming purchase in mind (a new bike, camera, computer, guitar, stereo or even a new pair of sneakers), older children might be enticed to consult guides for shoppers such as *Consumer Reports* or *Consumer Guide Magazine*. Most shopping guides not only provide useful information but also valuable practice in reading graphs and charts.

Don't conclude your library visit without encouraging your child to select some books for leisure reading. To help your child find books that relate to his or her particular interests, use the computer database or consult *Best Books for Children* (Fifth edition, R.R. Bowker, 1994). Here you'll find more than seventeen thousand titles arranged by subject including fairy tales, biographies of writers, stories about particular ethnic groups, books about circus life, astronomy, sports,

hobbies, mysteries, and so on. There is a brief description of each
book listed. If your library doesn't have a particular title you want,
check interlibrary loan or your local bookstore. *Best Books for Children* lists materials for kids from preschool through grade six. For
older children use its companion volume, *Best Books for Junior High
Readers.* Another good reference for children's books is *The New York
Times Parent's Guide to the Best Books for Children.* It categorizes books
by age and interest, including such headings as "adoption," "behavior problems," "fear," "death," "family problems," "minorities," and
"siblings."

Your library probably carries some of the major children's magazines. Those with circulation of more than five hundred thousand
include the following: *Muppet, Ranger Rick, Boys' Life, Barbie, Sesame
Street Magazine, Highlights for Children, Humpty Dumpty's Magazine,*
and *National Geographic World.*

You and your child can look in *Magazines for Young People* (published by R. R. Bowker) to find an extensive list of publications categorized by subject matter. If, after skimming through a magazine or
reading a description of one, your child indicates an interest in the
publication, consider subscribing. Magazines are a wonderful form
of enrichment.

Have fun at the library. Don't try to learn about everything in one
visit. As soon as one of you gets tired, quit for the day.

Computer Research

Kids and computers seem to go together like coffee and cream. Why?
The game-like quality makes it fun, and the anonymity is protective.
On-line, a student's age, acne, other perceived inadequacies—indeed,
the child's very identity—can be concealed. Moreover, if used correctly, the computer can become an extremely helpful homework
helper.

Having a home computer can be a great academic asset. And we
are moving toward a time when the home computer will be as standard a homework tool as the pencil. According to the Software Publishers Association, at least one-third of American households

possess a PC, and 70 percent of these have a modem, most with Internet access. But whether students have their own computers or not, all should become computer literate. (Summer courses are a good way to get kids really going on this skill.) If there's a computer at home, parents can help their children learn to use it. In many households the reverse occurs—the children teach the parents! The third wonderful possibility is for parents and kids to become computer literate together.

Students can use computers as homework helpers in so many ways. Here are just five of them: (1) They can use a word processing program to write papers. (2) They can use special programs to prepare art work, graphs, or other visuals to accompany their papers. (3) They can discuss homework assignments via E-mail. (4) They can use educational software programs to do research, study information, or practice academic skills. (5) They can do research on-line. Let's focus now on the research possibilities.

Students can consult a wide range of reference books via computer. Encyclopedias are available on CD-ROM or from an on-line service. Other references—such as a dictionary, an acronym dictionary, a thesaurus, Bartlett's *Familiar Quotations*—are also available on-line. America Online's Reference Desk gives users access to a wide range of reference materials.

One quick and easy way to find homework help on the Internet is via Mollie's Homework Helper (http://www.parkbank.com/ Dogpage.htm). Mollie is "an experienced Internet traveler." Her home page links to information on the arts, health and safety, history, language, mathematics, music, physical education, science, and social science. And each of those links takes you to a world of information about the subject. There are many more specific incantations for releasing a homework genie from your child's magical, mystical PC box. See the list of "Homework Help Websites" in the appendix of this book.

To find information when a specific Internet address is unknown, you can also use a search engine. Here are three of the most popular:

Yahoo! (http://www.yahoo.com)

Excite (http://www.excite.com)

AltaVista (http://www.altavista.digital.com)

After you have the search engine on the screen, type in a word or phrase describing the requested information. The engine will then return a list of sites matching the entered data.

There are also many useful Internet sites staffed by teachers and/or experts in a particular field that students can consult for assistance with specific homework problems. One of these is Homework Help (http://www.startribune.com/stonline/html/special/homework/). It offers teacher assistance in answering questions on virtually any topic. Here are a few more sites of this type described in Salzman and Pondiscio's *The Ultimate On-line Homework Helper*:

- The Academic Assistance Center (America Online)
  By entering the key word (AAC), students access this service and get four options: "Look it Up" (to search reference materials), "Live Help" (from tutors in various subject areas), "Ask a Teacher" (answers from tutors on-line), and "Explore" (to discover new ideas and interesting facts). The AAC also has Knowledge Database, a collection of hundreds of answers to previously asked questions. Another option: students can post questions on a message board.
- Internet Public Library (http://ipl.sils.umich.edu/)
  This site has a huge electronic catalog of reference works, a Youth section with a librarian eager to tackle homework questions, and a Teen section for older students.
- Dial-A-Teacher Online
  (http://tiger.chuh.cleveland-heights.k12.oh.us/)
  This service provides help with homework problems and gives advice on study strategies.

The *Ultimate On-line Homework Helper* is an extremely useful reference book for students who use a computer regularly. It gives sites to reach experts in several fields (such as "Ask Dr. Math," "Ask a Scientist," and "Ask a Doc"). There are many 1sites listed by academic subject. The book also tells students how to visit museums via cyberspace. Written in an entertaining style that appeals to young readers, this book describes itself as "the road to cyberspace . . . where homework is fun and learning is easy." What kid could resist embarking upon that journey? Three other books that can help kids navigate the Internet are listed at the end of this chapter.

But wait. Cyberspace researching is not always quick and easy. Getting homework answers on-line may take hours or even days. Sometimes the lines are busy; sometimes the experts are backlogged; sometimes the service is closed just when the student needs it. Although computerized homework assistance can be quite helpful at times, it should not be a student's only strategy for finding answers. We also recommend practice runs—using these homework sites when *not* facing a homework crisis. Encourage your child to make up a homework question, try it on several homework sites, see who answers quickly and correctly. Then he'll know which site(s) to use when faced with a real homework crisis.

Another warning: there's a lot of information on-line—and a lot of misinformation. Students need to be careful whose word they take. Advice about what medicine to give a goldfish might be coming from a ten-year-old who never even owned one.

Parents also worry about their kids' computer access to the wrong kind of information. Fortunately, today's technology makes it possible to allow kids access to the treasures of the Internet while restricting access to the slime. Screening software (such as SurfWatch) lets parents specify which Internet sites their children can access and blocks off all others.

A final warning: students can get too hooked up to the computer. It can become a way of life. Some young people live most of their out-of-school waking hours on-line instead of in the real world. Sitting at a computer night and day is not healthy for the body or the mind. Computer literacy, yes. Computer addiction, no. Children need to mingle with real people, to read books, and to get out and exercise. If your child isn't doing these things, you need to place limits upon his or her on-line life.

Talk Research: Using the Telephone

Besides using a modem, there are more traditional ways to use the telephone as a research tool. Does your child need to know why water expands when it freezes? A family friend who's a science teacher or an undergrad biology major should be able to provide an answer. Does the research question of the day involve a statistic, such as the population of the United States? If your child can't get to the local library, a reference librarian may supply the information by phone, or your local newspaper may have an information service to answer readers' questions.

The ultimate in telephone homework assistance is, of course, the homework helpline. In 1980 New York City created the prototype for this type of assistance with its free Dial-A-Teacher service. In the 1996–97 academic year Dial-A-Teacher handled about sixty thousand student calls! According to the project coordinator, Ira Dobren, this service (funded by the New York City Board of Education and the United Federation of Teachers) has a staff of forty-five teachers who can give homework help in several different languages. About 60 percent of the calls Dial-A-Teacher receives are related to mathematics. But whatever the subject, the teacher's goal is not to give the student the answer but to help the student discover how to find it for himself. During the academic year, the service operates from 4–7 P.M. Monday through Thursday evenings. To reach Dial-A-Teacher, kids can call (212) 777-3380. Adults who want further information about the service can call the office at (212) 598-9205 and ask for Ira Dobren or the Dial-A-Teacher director, Amina Rachman. Other cities offering similar phone services include Baltimore, Indianapolis, Wichita (Kansas), and New Haven (Connecticut).

One high school student we know astonished her U.S. history teacher with her telephone research resourcefulness. The class was asked to find an obscure piece of information: In 1775, when Ethan Allen seized Fort Ticonderoga from the British, he shouted, "Come out, you rat!" Who was the British commanding officer that surrendered without a fight? Marcia found the answer by calling the museum at Fort Ticonderoga. The phone numbers of major museums, historical sites, and national parks are easy to obtain from any travel guide book (such as *Fodor's '97 USA*) or from a phone operator if you know the city. Students who want a quick fact or more extensive information can ask to speak to a facility's historian, a tour guide at a site, or even a knowledgeable volunteer working in the visitors' center. On a regular basis, a long-distance approach to homework answers can add up to a big expense. But, in a pinch, it may be worth it. A question about the Wild West? It's exciting to talk to someone whose entire career is focused upon the development of the American West (such as the historian of the Museum of Westward Expansion beneath the Gateway Arch in St. Louis). If your child needs to know how much the last repair job on the Statue of Liberty cost, suggest calling the statue to find out. She's not likely to answer the phone herself, but one of her caretakers will probably supply the answer.

Dictionary Discoveries

Every school-age child should have an age-appropriate dictionary at home and should know how to use it. For grades one through five, a junior dictionary may suffice. By sixth grade or so, most students are ready to use a collegiate level desk-size dictionary for home reference. Encourage your older elementary student to become intimately acquainted with the dictionary she uses at home. (It may be organized somewhat differently from the one taught in school.)

How skillfully does your child use the dictionary? Find out by asking if your child can answer these questions: How are the definitions arranged? (Historical dictionaries put the earliest meaning first; dictionaries of common usage put the most common contemporary meaning first.) How does the dictionary indicate syllable division? Where is the key to the pronunciation symbols? Does your home dictionary put stress marks before or after the syllable to be stressed? Are proper nouns (people and places) integrated with common nouns or listed separately in the back of the dictionary? Encourage kids to read the introduction to the dictionary to learn how to use it. If that seems too hard, play around with a few words to illustrate how much information a dictionary contains and how easy that information is to access.

To practice dictionary skills, here are some questions older kids might find fun to look up:

- What are the meanings of the two word parts in *automobile* and *astronaut*?
- Why do we call a bound collection of maps an *atlas*? Who is the atlas named after?
- Is it correct or incorrect to pronounce the *t* in the word *often*? If two pronunciations are listed, which is the preferred one?
- What is the most common meaning of the word *segue*? How is it pronounced? What part(s) of speech can it be used as?
- Where does the stress go on these related words: *plethora* and *plethoric*?
- How do you spell the past tense forms of the verbs *prefer* and *bind*?
- Is the expression *rip off* slang, informal English, or standard English?
- What's the correct pronunciation of the word *extraordinary*?
- Do the words *disinterested* and *uninterested* mean the same thing?
- At the end of a line, where can you correctly hyphenate *transportation*? (Find three places.)

Parents can show kids that the dictionary puts a wealth of information literally at the reader's fingertips by keeping a good, recent dictionary handy and using it often.

When students become involved in doing research, they learn that truth can be evasive, that authors make errors, that different sources give different answers, that readers can't always trust a "fact" that appears in print or on the screen, that it's worthwhile to check more than one source. These are important lessons to learn.

Whatever the specific research task, a parent can be a mentor or a resource for how-to-do-it tips. But remember that the goal is not just to get the answer. It is also to help your child develop the know-how for finding information, experience the excitement of discovery, and build confidence in his ability to be a do-it-myself researcher.

About the Internet:
Books for Kids

Internet for Kids (second edition), Deneen Frazier. San Francisco: Sybex, 1996.
Sybex, Inc., 2001 Challenger Drive, Alameda, CA 94501

Librarian's Guide to Cyberspace for Parents & Kids (American Library Association, 1997). Includes a list of fifty great websites for children plus tips on how to stay safe on the Net.
ALA Public Information Office, Department P, 50 E. Huron Street, Chicago, IL 60611.
website: http://www.ala.org/parentspage/greatsites

World Wide Web for Kidz, Maggie Fisher. Stone Mountain, GA: GA Publishing, 1997. (800) 932-5439. (also available on CD-ROM)
website: http://www.4kidz.com

Reference Software

Merriam Webster Collegiate Dictionary (tenth edition). Integrated with thesaurus.
Zone Publishing, Inc. 1950 Stemons, Dallas, TX 75207, (214) 746-5555.

Microsoft Bookshelf (1996–97 edition). Provides access to nine of the latest reference works, including a dictionary, encyclopedia, and almanac.

CD-ROM Encyclopedias

The Complete Reference Collection
Compton's Interactive Encyclopedia
Encyclopedia Britannica World Book Multimedia Encyclopedia Deluxe

Eyewitness Children's Encyclopedia (with 20 virtual-reality environments)
Grolier Multimedia Encyclopedia
Microsoft Encarta

For Information About Educational Computer Software

Creative Wonders: (800) 543-9778
Crimson Multimedia Distribution, Inc.: (800) 989-4084
Edmark: (800) 362-2890
The Learning Company: (800) 227-5609
Microsoft: (800) 426-9400

Locating Reviews of Educational Software on the Internet

ESI Online Educational Software Catalog
http://esi.cuesta.com/www/esicat/@MWys11bmPR.ho/search.html

Software Evaluation Selection Page for Education
http://baddog.sp.utoledo.edu/~lelsie/StudF96/dricken/software.html

Superkids Educational Software Review
http://www.superkids.com/aweb/pages/contents.html

11

Providing Enrichment in Math, Social Studies, and Science

Please Don't Force-Feed the Children!

Remember the joke about the boy scout who got beaten up trying to help an old lady across the street? Trouble was, she didn't want to go. Neither do children who are forced along a particular academic path.

Joe wants his ten-year old son to take over the family accounting practice someday, so he pushes the boy into an accelerated math program. Gail, a science teacher who wishes she had become a doctor, hopes her children will fulfill her dreams, so she's got her reluctant offspring hovering over a microscope. Anything wrong with these situations? You bet. We're talking about two toxic types of parents here: (1) those who identify too closely with their children, who see their children as younger versions of themselves; and (2) those who see their children as an opportunity to relive their lives but get it right this time. In other words, the children are expected to accomplish what the parent couldn't or didn't. By sharing their love of a particular kind of work, parents often inspire their children to pursue the same career. But pointing the way is a lot different from pushing the child down the path. Enrichment in academic subject areas should not be used to steer children in a particular occupational direction. It should not narrow career options but expand them.

Successful enrichment can make what's taught in school more relevant and interesting to students. But no family has the time, resources, or interest to provide enrichment in every academic area. The enrichment suggestions given in this book are intended as *coulds* not *shoulds*.

Mathematics

Who's mathematically gifted? Don't be too quick to jump to conclusions and apply labels. Mathematics utilizes a number of skills, and a student can be more adept at some and less adept at others. Some children are careful workers and can add up long columns of numbers and get the right answer. Some children have good memories and process information quickly, so they can shoot back basic math facts (such as $9 \times 7 = 63$) with the rapidity of a calculator. Some children are especially good at the problem-solving aspects of math. Some kids can think creatively with numbers and notice numerical patterns and relationships that no one has ever taught them. Some kids have visual ability that makes geometry easy for them.

Parents who know the general goals of their children's math instruction for the current year are better able to provide related enrichment. How to find out? Look at your child's math textbook, go to meetings at the school and, if information about the math curriculum is not given, ask for a list or an oral rundown of what's covered. For each grade level there may be fifteen or more topics. Most fit under one of these headings: numbers, arithmetic (including fractions, percent, and decimals), measurement (including time, distance, and amount), comparisons, patterns (numerical and geometric), and probability and statistics.

If you ask your child about his or her math lessons, you may find the activities quite different from what went on in your school days. Today there is less emphasis upon rote learning and more emphasis upon problem-solving skills. Children are learning that good mathematical thinking involves a wide range of problem-solving strategies, including intelligent guessing.

The goals of math enrichment should be (1) to help children realize that math is an important part of adult life not only on the job but in personal activities as well; and (2) to help children develop a can-do and a want-to-do attitude about math (to feel that they are capable of understanding it and that the challenge can be fun). Both goals are important, whether the child is a boy or a girl.

To help kids relate to math better, there are several things parents can do:

Call attention to everyday math applications. Parents can help children notice math applications—the use of math in everyday life—by involving kids in conversations about calculations. How big a tip should we leave in a restaurant? What's the price of this shirt on sale for 20 percent off? How long will it take us to drive to Philadelphia? Encourage kids to work out these calculations independently or with a little parental guidance.

Remember the power of money. Perhaps the easiest way to entice kids into using math is by giving them some responsibility for the handling of money. Children should have the same kinds of experiences with money that adults do—earning, saving, spending, and perhaps even borrowing (combined with the payback of the loan). All school-age children should get an allowance, make small purchases for themselves from time to time, and learn to count the change they get. By the intermediate grades, children are ready to handle an allowance that covers their expenses for school supplies and recreation. In addition to an allowance, kids often get money as payment for occasional jobs and as gifts. They should be encouraged to save some of their "income"—to open a bank account with a particular financial goal in mind (such as saving for a new bike or for college tuition). At grammar school graduation time, some children receive enough gift money to buy stock. Doing so provides an excellent learning opportunity, especially if the kids are involved in the choice of stock purchased and learn how to follow its price fluctuations.

Estimate and guesstimate. Adults do it all the time. In fact, we couldn't function well if we didn't. How much longer will it take me to get to work today in this snowstorm? How much is this dinner bill going to be? How many hot dogs will I need for the birthday barbecue? Throughout our daily activities, we make estimates, and then we make decisions based upon these estimates. If our estimates turn out to be too high or too low, we note that and adjust our thinking when a similar estimate is needed in the future. Estimates help us catch errors, our own and others'. If a restaurant bill is $15 too high, we'll notice if we've estimated the total.

Estimating is an important skill for children to learn, an important habit to get into. Parents can encourage this kind of thinking by involving children in their own estimating processes. ("How much do you think these groceries will cost? Do you think I can pay for them with this $20 bill, or will I have to write a check?" "What time should we leave for your friend's house? How long do you think it will take to get there?") Before doing a math problem for school, a student should estimate the answer. Then, a number very far from that will be a red flag, an indication that the answer doesn't make sense, and that it's necessary to do the problem again. Asked to estimate the sum of $11/12 + 12/13$, a student shouldn't begin searching for the common denominator. The student should know that, when the numerator and denominator are close in value, each fraction equals about one. So the quick, estimated answer to this question is, "About 2."

Talk about the language of mathematics. Like any academic field, math has its own vocabulary. Parents can help kids learn it by asking kids what "math words" they are using in class and whether they can define or explain them. Sometimes parents can suggest ways to keep new words straight. For example, the word *parallel* has three parallel letter l's in it. The word *perimeter*—the outside boundary of a closed figure—contains the word part *peri-* which means "around." (Your child may be familiar with a periscope, a device used for looking around the surface of the water from a submarine.)

Make math fun and games. Believe it or not, math can be fun. Try to come up with some challenging math questions that your child can mull over, and be willing to put your brain to work on any that your child brings home to you. For example, to practice seeing numerical patterns, ask your child to figure out the next number in the following series:

42, 43, 45, 48, 52, _____
(The answer is 57—add 1, then 2, then 3, etc.)

How about this one? 93, 39, 61, 16, 14, _____
(The answer is 41—just reverse the digits.)

An entertaining math activity can be initiated using something as simple as a straight line. With younger children, the straight line might be labeled this way:

0 _____24

The task can be to write in all the whole numbers, the even (or odd) numbers, or every third number. Once your child has been introduced to fractions or decimals, label the line as follows and try these questions:

0_____1

"Can you put these fractions on the line in ascending order: 1/6; 1/5; 3/4; 1/2; 5/8; 5/6? Where on the line would .5 go? Where would .75 go? What other decimals could you put on the line? What is the largest decimal we could put on this line? (.99999, etc.) What is the smallest? How many decimals can we put on the line?" Next, change the digits to 0 and 2 and ask your child to write in the number closest to 1.

For challenging, entertaining problems that involve thinking (not mere calculating), look into *Math for Smarty Pants* by Marilyn Burns. Here's a problem from her book. (It can be solved with simple addition or subtraction; still, many adults get it wrong.) A boy buys a bicycle for $40, sells it for $50, buys it back for $60, and sells it for $70. Did he make or lose money? How much? (The answer: he made $20. You can think this out in many different ways. For example, he was involved in two buying and selling transactions and made $10 on each; he spent a total of $100 on his purchases and received a total of $120 on the sales, giving him a $20 profit.)

There are many good books that teach a wide range of mathematical concepts in an entertaining, sometimes narrative way. (See the list at the end of this chapter.) These can be family fun, even dinnertable conversation. When doing math games with your child, try not to give away the answer. Instead, provide enough clues to enable your child to come up with the solution. If necessary, do a similar problem together (change the digits); then let your child do the original one independently and enjoy the feeling of being a mathematical success. Don't let family math games discourage a younger or less mathematically adept child. If sibling rivalry becomes a factor in your family's math games, then don't do them as a group but instead in a one-on-one parent-child situation.

Computer software also makes math fun (or, at least, more fun) for kids. What to buy? Read reviews in computer magazines and/or ask software salespeople, teachers, other parents, and kids for advice. To find Internet reviews of new software, consult the sites listed at the end of Chapter 10. Two very popular pieces of math software are *Math Blaster*, which includes four math games and about fifty thousand different problems, and *Math Workshop*, which includes a disk containing information for parents about how to help youngsters learn and enjoy math.

Use visuals and manipulatives. What's the difference between 3 × 6 and 6 × 3? The product is the same, but the groupings are not. That becomes clear when a child manipulates raisins into three groups of six and then six groups of three. Children "get" math concepts more easily when they can see, move, and use things. Kids can learn about geometric shapes by using them in puzzles or building their own with toothpicks and marshmallows. A math problem may be easier to understand when the information is placed on a graph.

Metric measurements become more meaningful when a child cooks something using metric measuring cups and spoons.

Social Studies

Social studies is primarily about people—how and where they live now or lived in the past. Social studies enrichment should begin by teaching children who they are and where they fit into the social structure. Children should have a sense of their own identity. To achieve this, they need to know about their family history, community, ethnic, and religious background, and national heritage. Once they have an understanding of their own background, children are able to compare and contrast their own culture with others. Parents can help children develop interests in what has happened or is happening beyond their own small world. Here are some ways to do that:

Bring the world into your home. Talk about places far and near, and accompany these discussions with maps. Keep these three maps handy—a map of your community, of the United States, and of the world. Be sure your child can find his street, city, state, and country on the various maps. Older children can be asked to make a map showing guests from out of town or across town how to reach their home. When a city or country is discussed—either because it's in the news or because someone in the family is going there—ask your child to find that place on the map.

Enriching geographical experiences abound. Children can put together a large floor map puzzle of the United States. (These are sold in parent-teacher stores.) And students eight and older love to study geography via the Carmen Sandiego mystery geography series, available in board games and computer software. The series includes "Where in the World Is Carmen Sandiego?" "Where in the USA Is Carmen Sandiego?" "Where in Europe Is Carmen Sandiego?" and "Where in Time Is Carmen Sandiego?"

Explore cultures outside your own. Go to a Buddhist temple, an Indian reservation, an Amish community, and so on. (To get a good understanding of the Amish way of life, get an audiotape about the Amish, and play it while driving through the eastern part of Lancaster County, Pennsylvania. About five million people a year make this fascinating tour.) Help children recognize the ways in which people are different and the ways in which they are similar.

Visit sites that recreate a historical period. Time travel seems almost possible when we take advantage of facilities that have re-created or preserved past cultures. If your community or a nearby one has a Medieval Fair, it's worth checking out. (Remember to provide advanced organizers for the excursion by talking or reading about that historical period first.) There are many wonderful places for reliving American history. Here are some of our favorites:

- Colonial Williamsburg: Virginia's eighteenth-century capital city has been restored to re-create the atmosphere on the eve of the American Revolution. On this 173-acre site there are 88 original structures, hundreds of colonial reconstructions, and costumed interpreters to tell about colonial life in Williamsburg.
- Plimoth Plantation: a reconstruction of Plymouth Colony in Massachusetts as it looked in 1627. Here kids can meet properly attired Pilgrims and visit their homes. Plan ahead, and you can even have Thanksgiving dinner at Plimoth Plantation.
- Amana Colonies: a living museum with seven rustic villages and more than four hundred original nineteenth-century structures. Visitors to this Iowa site learn about the communal way of life a group of German immigrants once shared.

For further information about historical sites, consult the latest *Fodor's USA* guidebook or the *National Geographic Guide to America's Historic Places*. The latter features more than twenty-five hundred U.S. historical sites including battlefields, Wild West towns, colonial villages, and Indian dwellings.

Use videos to teach about cultures. Many excellent movies that depict the lifestyle and philosophies of various cultures are available on videotape. Find one that ties in with what your child is studying in social studies class, and watch it together.

Use resources from a time or place being studied in school.
If your son is studying World War II, have him talk to Great-uncle Harry, a World War II veteran. If your daughter is studying the Far East, a visit to an Asian neighborhood would be enlightening.

Science

Jon D. Miller, a researcher in scientific illiteracy, studied seven thousand students in junior high, high school, and college to find out how they acquired scientific knowledge. His conclusion? "Parents account for it 8 times out of 10," he told *Chicago Tribune* science writer Ronald Kotulak. "Parents drive the system." Enrichment in the sciences can be as serene as birdwatching on your block or as scary as concocting a mysterious bubbly liquid in a test tube. As with other enrichment, scientific enrichment can be inspired by a parent's hobby or a child's question. Scientific enrichment can encourage kids to observe, to wonder why, and to seek correct answers by using logic, experimentation, and evidence. You and your child can accomplish these goals with the following activities.

Do science experiments at home. On a 1996 national science test given to 123,000 American students, kids did poorly on the section that asked them to design an experiment. For example, only 12 percent of fourth graders realized that, to find out if beetles prefer light or shade, they would need to place water dishes in both the lighted and shaded sides of the beetles' box, not just on one side. Parents can help kids learn about scientific methods of discovery by doing simple experiments with them. Libraries and stores for parents and teachers are good places to find books of experiments that can be performed at home with ordinary, inexpensive materials. Let children choose some experiments that interest them and then design some experiments of their own.

Encourage participation in school science fairs. Science-fair preparation can be hectic and nerve-wracking for parents. As part of three different school science fair projects, one household we know of had fruit flies (in test tubes) in the kitchen, mold (in closed containers) in the refrigerator, and earthworms (in dirt-filled aquariums) in the rec room.

Science fairs present a difficult homework dilemma. Most are competitive, and parental involvement is almost a prerequisite for being a prize winner. However, too much help means the child winds up being lauded for the parent's work. One mother tells of being pulled three ways at once: she was giving project advice to her oldest son while helping her second son put together his display board. Meanwhile, her third son was pulling on her skirt and saying, "Mommy, when are you going to start on *my* science fair project?" Yes, work with your child on a science fair project, but be the assistant, not the boss. Enjoy the process, take pride in the effort, and play down the prizes. (Some sources for science fair project ideas are listed at the end of this chapter.)

Go sight-seeing. Museums, planetariums, aquariums, zoos, safari parks, caves, mountains, or woods—there's no shortage of scientific sites, indoors and out. In San Francisco? Visit the Exploratorium (a wonderful interactive museum) or drive up to the Muir Woods to stand beside the gigantic Redwoods. In Los Angeles? Check out the Griffith Park Observatory's laser light show and the La Brea Tar Pits (one of the world's richest sources of Ice Age fossils). In Chicago? Visit the Museum of Science and Industry. Every child should have direct experiences with nature—see a mountain, explore a cave, hike through a forest, swim in an ocean, see marine life up close. For spectacular cave exploration, visit Mammoth Cave in Kentucky or Carlsbad Caverns in New Mexico. Observe marine life at some amazing facilities—Sea World in San Diego, the National Aquarium in Baltimore, the Aquarium of the Americas in New Orleans, or the Shedd Aquarium in Chicago. Take advantage of the interesting places within driving distance of your home, and, when you travel farther away, try to fit in some scientific sites that cross your path. Wherever you visit, purchase a book about the site so that you and your children can review the experience at home.

In deciding where to go, ask for some input from your children. Choose a site that you and/or they feel enthusiastic about seeing. Michael Shermer's *Teach Your Child Science* has an eleven-page list of science and nature museums by region and state. Larry Ludmer's *The Great American Wilderness: Touring America's National Parks* describes forty-one areas administered by the National Park Service. For evaluations from people who have been there, consult *Consumer Reports* (June 1997). This special outdoor issue focuses on the best national parks, monuments, and recreational areas, summarizing data from forty thousand tourists, including descriptions, evaluations, and complaints.

Encourage scientific hobbies. Pets and plants are great. (Cuong trained his pet guinea pig to fetch a pencil. Carlita grew what looked like the world's largest radish in her back yard.) Some hobbies require expensive equipment—a telescope or a microscope, for example. Invest in these items only after your child has demonstrated a serious interest in using them.

Consider a magazine subscription. Skim some science magazines for kids, and see which one best suits your child's reading level and area of interest. Your local library probably has copies of most of these: *Chickadee*, *National Geographic World*, *Odyssey*, *Owl*, *Ranger Rick's Nature Magazine Monthly*, and *Scienceland*.

Observe science in action. What's growing in your neighborhood? Go out and take a look. Any major events in the sky? Don't let a comet or an eclipse go by without your inspection. Show an interest in the science around you, and share it with your child.

Check out the latest computer software. These days, computer programs in the sciences are scientific wonders themselves. For example, Microsoft's *The Magic School Bus Explores the Rain Forest* provides multimedia, interactive science adventures. Kids can play fourteen science-based games, adjust the temperature and rainfall of a habitat, alter the pitch of a frog's song, even ride on a humming-bird's back. Consider science CD-ROMs for gifts.

Teach good health habits. The most important science enrichment that the home can provide concerns eating properly and exercising regularly. How to teach these things? By example!

Share _Infinity_ with your child. The 1996 film _Infinity_ (directed by and starring Broderick Crawford and available on videotape) is well worth watching with an older child. It tells the poignant true story of a Nobel prize-winning physicist (Richard Feynman), who worked at Los Alamos on the development of the atomic bomb. In the film viewers see scientific curiosity at work and play and also see the joy and strength that Feynman derives from his scientific approach to life.

Additional Resources

Books

For enrichment in math:

Family Math, Jean Kerr Stenmark, Virginia Thompson, and Ruth Cossey. Berkeley, University of California, 1996. To order a copy, write: Lawrence Hall of Science, University of California, Berkeley, CA 94720

How to Develop Your Child's Gifts and Talents in Math, Ronn Yablun. Los Angeles: RGA Publishing Group, Inc., 1995.

30 Wild and Wonderful Math Stories to Develop Problem-Solving Skills, Dan Greenberg. New York: Scholastic Professional Books, 1992.

For enrichment in social studies:

American Places: A Writer's Pilgrimage to 15 of This Country's Most Visited and Cherished Sites, William Zinsser. New York: HarperCollins Publishers, 1992.

For enrichment in science:

50 Nifty Super Science Experiments, Lisa Melton and Eric Ladizinsky. Los Angeles: Lowell House, 1997.

My First Science Fair Projects, Q. L. Pearce. Los Angeles: Lowell House, 1997.

Teach Your Child Science: Making Science Fun for Both of You, Michael Shermer. Los Angeles: Lowell House, 1995.

Websites for Math, Social Studies, and Science

If your child's math course is beyond your knowledge, why not Ask Dr. Math (http://forum.swarthmore.edu/dr.math/)?

For social studies, everything you ever wanted to know about the countries of the world is contained in the CIA World Factbook. (http://www.odci.gov/cia/publications/nsolo/wfb-all.htm).

For information on national parks and historic sites, consult the National Park Service's ParkNet Web page (http://www.nps.gov), an Internet guide to all the national parks and historic sites.

Tips about science fair projects can be found by typing in *sciencefair* on a search engine (such as Yahoo!, AltaVista, or Excite) to get a list of sites. Also check out the Science Fair link at Cyberspace Middle School (http://www.scri.fsu.edu/~dennisl/CMS.html).

Additional Source for Science Fair Project Ideas

The Learning Tree (Gray's Distributing, Inc.) 1997–98 Educational Materials Catalog: (800) 688-2959; On-line: http://www.edumart. com/thelearningtree

12

Providing Enrichment in the Language and Performing Arts

Reading

Reading is the most important academic skill because nearly all other schoolwork depends upon it. Parents are understandably concerned when they hear that one out of five schoolchildren is reading-impaired by fourth grade. To avoid becoming a part of such a statistic, a child with suspected reading problems should receive a professional evaluation immediately. The longer intervention is delayed, the longer it takes to make up deficits.

Many parents remain involved with their children's reading only in the early grades, when kids are struggling with decoding (recognizing words). But reading enrichment can also be quite beneficial in the middle and upper elementary grades. Remember that reading is a lot more than decoding. In fact, some children (called *hyperlexic*) are super decoders at an early age but have poor reading comprehension. To understand what is read, the student needs to comprehend word meanings, ideas, and relationships between ideas. Through activities at home parents can help with all these. The goals of reading enrichment are (1) to get kids to read more; (2) to improve comprehension; and (3) to help kids find pleasure in leisure reading so that it will become a life-long habit. To move toward these goals, we make the following recommendations:

Model the behavior you want your child to exhibit. Be a regular reader yourself. Read in front of your child. Share interesting tidbits about what you learned from your reading. Subscribe to a daily newspaper and a weekly news magazine. If these are around the house and your child sees you perusing them with interest, chances are your child will pick them up too.

Read together. That might involve everyone seated in the living room, reading different materials but sharing a quiet reading time and space. Or it might be a weekly oral reading session with family members reading aloud to one another, sharing things they've recently read and enjoyed. Reading sessions can also be formalized around themes: poetry, sports, humor, etc. Some families read short stories or plays aloud. Some schools and public libraries establish mother/daughter and father/son book clubs to encourage family members to read and discuss some of the same books.

In selecting reading materials to share, you might begin with authors you enjoyed as a child. For further ideas consult our list of suggested books (by grade level) in the appendix. For reading materials in various subject areas, take a look at the *Core Knowledge Series*, edited by E. D. Hirsch Jr., the author of *Cultural Literacy*. The series includes books for kindergarten through grade six (volumes are entitled *What Your Kindergartner Needs to Know* and so on). The Core Knowledge series contains wonderful material—short stories, excerpts from novels, poetry, and mythology, plus reading materials on the sciences and social sciences—written at a level appropriate for each grade. Many school and public libraries carry the Core Knowledge Series.

Read what your child recommends. If your child loved a particular book and wants you to read it too, find time to read at least some of it, and then discuss it with your child. It's an opportunity to discover what your child got out of the reading and to share your adult perspective. But avoid uninvited shadowing of your child's reading choices. That may be viewed as an invasion of privacy. Before dipping into your child's library, ask if it's okay.

Put leisure-reading time on your child's schedule. Besides reading for school, children should do some reading for pleasure. When there's no homework, study time may be used for leisure reading. However, additional time for reading (perhaps 30 minutes per day) should be included in a child's weekly schedule. As is the case with other hobbies, leisure reading offers these benefits: (1) it provides a release from academic stress; (2) practice leads to improvement. The regular reader becomes a better reader.

Encourage vocabulary development. English has the largest vocabulary of any language, so vocabulary study can (and should) be a life-long endeavor. Learn new words yourself. Tell your child about a new word you learned recently. Ask what new words your child learned that week. Play word games and do crossword puzzles. Keep a dictionary handy to settle debates about word meanings. Dictionary consultation is especially important for bilingual students who may be trying to get by with only vague ideas of what more difficult words mean or who may be tricked by false cognates into attributing the wrong meaning to a word. Also encourage kids to make intelligent guesses about word meanings by studying context clues; this is an important reading skill.

Help your kids become skilled at nonprose reading. Take advantage of real-life opportunities to show your child how to read a road map, an airplane ticket, a bus or train schedule, a chart, or a graph.

Help your children notice subtleties in language usage. Good reading involves such skills as grasping inferences, understanding figurative language, seeing cause and effect, recognizing contrasting ideas, and understanding irony. When you share and discuss reading materials with your child, you have an opportunity to talk about the development of ideas. But these aspects of language usage can also be noted and analyzed as they occur in conversation. For example, one father got his daughter thinking about inferences and implications with this conversation: "I asked your mother if she liked this tie with this suit, and she said, 'Don't you have a blue tie?' What do you think she meant by that?"

Tape stories for younger children. Kids in the primary grades enjoy listening to audiotapes of their favorite stories while following along with the book. A parent or older sibling can make the tapes, and the child can enjoy being read to and reading simultaneously.

Writing

One community college English teacher began a writing class by asking students to define *good writing*. To her dismay, the students said that good writing meant writing without spelling and punctuation errors! What's a better definition? Good writing says something interesting in an interesting way. Children need to think of the message as most important and the mechanics as useful devices to help convey the message. It's sad when the child who has trouble with mechanics—spelling, punctuating, capitalizing—comes home from school believing "I'm a lousy writer." Writing is something people must do all their lives, so it's important to make children feel comfortable and confident about their abilities in this area.

Many children won't allow their parents to read their school essays either because they are ashamed of them or because they don't want parents telling them how and what to write. In attempting to guide students toward better writing, parents must be careful. Writing is the most personal of all academic endeavors. When adults are adversely critical of a child's thoughts on paper, the child is likely to feel insulted and belittled. So don't take a red pen to your child's writing. Instead, encourage your child to become his own editor. Point out that good writing is achieved by rewriting. (A public relations copywriter we know has this sign above her desk: "You mean you want the revised revision of the revised revision revised?!") Suggest rereading school essays at least three times, each time for a different purpose, first for development of ideas, then for sentence structure, and, finally, for mechanics (such as spelling and punctuation).

People write for two main reasons: to express their feelings and to communicate with others. (Of course, these writing goals often overlap.) Parents can encourage children to write at home to accomplish various purposes and to find audiences (besides their teachers) for their writing. Here are a few suggestions:

Establish a "family suggestion box." If kids want the family to buy something, go somewhere, do something, or change some household rule, they can write out their suggestions, which will then be taken up at a family meeting.

Encourage the use of writing to express thoughts, feelings, and desires. Boris is angry with his mother because she has taken his bicycle away for a week (to punish him for leaving it outside unlocked). "That's not fair!" Boris yells. "Put your complaint in writing," his mother says. Children who are encouraged to put their feelings on paper get writing practice along with a chance to work out their frustrations.

Encourage journal keeping. It may be on paper (in a diary) or on the computer. It need not be a daily activity but perhaps a twice-a-week habit. Children might be asked to share some portion of what they have written with the family, if they want to. This is an opportunity for giving encouraging feedback such as "I know just how you feel" or "That was a funny incident, and you described it well."

Enlist a younger child's help with your writing tasks. Even in the primary grades, children can write for real purposes. While Gloria was doing the dishes, she asked her daughter to write out the next day's grocery list, telling her the items to write down, asking for suggestions from her daughter, and helping a little with the spelling. Gloria also asked for her daughter's help in composing a letter to Aunt Sophie: "What family news can you think of that I can tell Aunt Sophie about?"

Encourage kids to write letters that they actually mail—or E-mail. They might write to request a favorite basketball player's photo, to suggest an idea to the President, to get information about a trip to Disneyland, etc. When they get a response, they experience success with their writing.

Encourage writing on a computer. On a computer, writing is more fun, revising is almost painless, and creativity is encouraged. Kids can even write interactive stories with a variety of possible endings by using a database program such as *Hyperstudio*.

Suggest finding a computer key pal. Pen pals may sound old-fashioned, but key pals are definitely "in." To locate key pal sites, just go to a Web search engine (such as Yahoo!, AltaVista, or Excite) and type in "key pal."

Suggest putting out a newspaper or newsletter. Kids' newspapers—containing jokes, movie reviews, student art work and puzzles, and school news—can be quite popular in a classroom or around the neighborhood. Newsletters about a particular topic (for example, hobbies or sports) can also be a hit. These days, computer word processing and photocopying make it easy to turn a child into a newspaper editor or columnist. Doing so can inspire an interest and build confidence in writing.

Suggest becoming a biographer. Encourage a child to spend some time with a beloved elderly family member and write up that person's biography. It can be given to other family members as a gift. Questions for the interview can be written up on the computer. Then, after the interview, the answers can be filled in on the computer.

Encourage submissions to publications. The magazine *Highlights for Children* publishes stories and poems (as well as art work) created by kids. Children can submit work to this or other children's magazines. Youngsters with strong opinions can also write to their local newspapers. Encourage entering writing contests. Getting published helps a child feel that writing is something he or she can do successfully.

Provide a tape recorder and suggest writing a dialogue. This activity requires only two kids, a conflict situation, and some imagination. The actors can improvise their dialogue, tape record it, play it back, revise it, recite it again, and, once they're satisfied with their "script," write it out or put it on the computer. The final product can then be performed for family or friends.

Encourage free voluntary reading (FVR). No doubt about it—research assures us that reading improves writing. Stephen Krashen makes this point emphatically in his book *The Power of Reading*. As Krashen tells his readers, reading improves prose style, spelling, and even grammar. Clearly, more exposure to the written word leads to improvement in its use. Therefore, we reiterate: be sure that your child develops the habit of pursuing interests via reading. Be sure leisure reading gets some solid blocks of time on your child's weekly schedule.

Spelling

Using the spelling word *umbrella*, Barbara, a second grader, wrote the following sentence: "An umbrella keeps me warm."

"Does it?" her teacher asked.

"No," said the little girl. "But I didn't know how to spell *dry*."

No one wants concerns about correct spelling to stifle written communication in this fashion, so it's important to be patient about a child's spelling progress. It isn't easy to spell correctly in English because (unlike Spanish) it's not a simple matter of one spelling, one sound. Vowels are especially difficult. Think of *ou* in *enough*, *out*, *cough*, and *coup*. Think of *ea* in *treat*, *break*, and *bread*. Remember that in unstressed syllables, the vowel sound is often reduced to *uh*, so the sound doesn't tell the speaker how to spell the word. It's easy to forget that the last vowel in *common* is an *o*, not an *e* or *i*. How can parents help?

Use games. Where spelling is concerned, playing with words really pays off, so get into the game mode. Ghost is a great game for a car ride because it's oral. (The goal is to avoid adding a letter that completes a word.) To pass the time on a plane ride, play Hangman. (If you don't know how to play, ask your child to teach you.) The old standbys Scrabble and Boggle are also fun. Stores and catalogs for parents and teachers have a wide selection of other games for practicing spelling. You can also make up your own. These can be very simple. For example, in two minutes who can make the longest list of words containing a silent *u* after *g* (*guest*, *guarantee*, etc.)? Or in three minutes make two lists, one with *ie* words and the other with *ei* words. Which list would you expect would be longer? Which list was longer for most players? Who had the most words (correctly spelled, of course)?

Call attention to the meanings of word parts. For example, remind your child that *full* is a complete word. When using the suffix that means "full of," the spelling is *-ful* (as in *careful*). Once children learn that the prefix *syn-* means "with" or "together," they're less likely to think that *synchronize* begins with *sin*.

Talk about homophones. Homophones are words that sound alike but are different in meaning and often different in spelling also. (For example, *wait* and *weight* are homophones). They are a common source of spelling errors. Remind your child that his computer spell check is oblivious to these kinds of errors. If your child is willing, discuss one pair each weekday and review on the weekends. Make it into a game by giving clues and asking the child to guess the pair and then to use each word in a sentence. Ask your child to list the homophones she knows. Add to the list weekly. Provide a reward for progress.

Severe, chronic spelling problems may be an indication of a learning disability. For more information about learning disabilities, see Chapter 13.

Foreign Languages

Enrichment for foreign language study is largely a matter of giving the child nonacademic opportunities to use the language and become better acquainted with the culture(s) that speak that language. For example, if your child is studying Spanish, you can do the following:

- Take the family to a Spanish restaurant, chat with the server, and ask about the meanings of the Spanish words on the menu.
- Contact a native (or fluent) Spanish speaker, and arrange for your child to have weekly phone conversations with that person.
- Take your child to see Spanish language movies or rent Spanish videos to watch at home.
- Go to shops, museum exhibits, festivals, shows, etc., featuring Hispanic products and performances.
- Consider taking a family trip to a Spanish-speaking country, or sending your child to a Spanish-speaking country with a school group.
- Suggest that your child correspond with a Spanish-speaking computer key pal.

If you speak the language your child is learning, use it in conversation with your child for at least fifteen minutes a day. If you don't, ask your child to teach you a few phrases or tell you a little about how this language differs from English.

The Performing Arts

Enrichment in the arts is most enjoyably achieved by attending performances. These don't have to be expensive. Kids don't need to see professional productions. Take advantage of community and high school productions—plays, concerts, and dance shows. Seeing other young people perform often inspires kids to get involved in the arts themselves. And even if that doesn't happen, learning to enjoy and appreciate the arts is valuable. Remember advanced organizers. Prepare children for what they are going to see onstage by talking about it, playing the music, or reading some of the text.

Private or group lessons in music, dance, and drama are also wonderful forms of enrichment. They are most effective when children are allowed to pursue their own interests and talents, not their parents' dreams for them.

Some Final Thoughts on Enrichment

Schools chop knowledge into academic subject areas. Parents can help kids see connections. Let's call it *interdisciplinary enrichment*. When a child is studying geometric shapes in math class, it's fun to look for cubes, spheres, cylinders, and cones in Cubist art or for various kinds of angles in stained glass windows. If a student is studying World War II in history class, parents can enrich that experience by exposing kids to the music, movies, and magazines of the early 1940s. Are your kids studying inventors? The lives of Thomas Alva Edison and the Wright brothers teach not merely science but the history of their era and the value of perseverance. A visit to the North Carolina site of the Wright brothers' first flight or to Edison's New Jersey lab gives students a glimpse into a great mind. Is European history in this year's curriculum? Talk about Copernicus and Galileo with your children. Their stories teach students science, history, religion, and courage. What happens when new knowledge contradicts accepted views? It is a problem every generation and every field of study faces, and parents can discuss this with kids.

Enrichment of children's academic experiences occurs spontaneously in most households. If parents take time to ask about what's going on in school, they can usually respond with some new insights for children—something that ties one subject to another, ties academics to real life, and ties adult concerns to children's interests. These are some of the major goals of academic enrichment.

Additional Resources

Books

How to Develop Your Child's Gifts and Talents in Writing, Martha Cheney. Los Angeles: Lowell House, 1997.

Parent Letters for the Intermediate Grades, edited by Karen P. Hall. Cypress, CA: Creative Teaching Press, Inc., 1997.

Tapes

To rent tapes for students who have difficulty reading printed material due to visual, physical, or perceptual impairment, contact

Talking Tapes/Textbooks on Tape
16 Sunnen Drive, Suite 162, St. Louis, MO 63143-3800
Phone: (314) 646-0500; Fax: (314) 646-0555

13

Answering Parents' Questions

"Inadequate" Homework

My son puts little or no effort into his homework. Is there anything I can say or do to get him to work harder?

Sometimes parents make hasty, inaccurate assumptions about effort. They may not know when a child puts a lot of effort into something. They may not know which assignments the teacher expects students to put a lot of effort into. Unless the teacher tells you that your son is not putting enough effort into his schoolwork, don't get involved. If the teacher feels the effort is inadequate, the first logical step would be for the *teacher* to talk to the *child* about the problem. Parents should not, on their own, evaluate schoolwork and decide that it was produced without effort and is inadequate.

My daughter, a fourth grader, does her homework very quickly and turns in very messy work. When I tell her to copy papers over so that they are neater, she tells me her teacher doesn't care. How can I get her to take more pride in her work?

Again, as in the situation discussed above, beware of pervasive intervention. If the teacher doesn't care that the work is messy, why should you? If you want your daughter to rake the leaves or make her bed in a neat fashion, these are your opportunities to teach neatness. Schoolwork is the teacher's domain. Perhaps, compared to other fourth graders, her work isn't all that messy. Even if it is, be patient. Your daughter's work may get neater as her coordination improves with age or when she gets a teacher who won't accept sloppy work.

Are some kids just lazy? If so, is there anything parents can do about it? My son is entering high school in the fall. He's never put much effort into schoolwork. He's always done the minimum and gotten average grades. Is there any way I can light a fire under him, or is it too late?

No child is inherently lazy. (But if you frequently scold a child for being lazy, you may get a passive-aggressive response in the form of "lazy" behavior.) The "lazy" label is a misnomer applied to a child who doesn't want to do something that the adults in his life want him to do. This dangerous, vague, catch-all term describes no specific behavior. The person who labels someone as lazy is usually angry because of an inability to control the so-called "lazy" person.

There's also no such thing as "too late"—not in school, not in therapy, not even on one's deathbed. Change is always possible. How can you "light a fire" under your son? You can't. You can talk about his goals and how effort now will help him to accomplish them. It can't hurt, but don't count on the success of this approach. Helping him to find goals via new interests, new experiences, and the development of his abilities may help, too. But there are no magic pills that parents can give kids to make them compliant or academically ambitious. Patience, encouragement, and enthusiasm for education are the best "magic" we have to offer. Contracts can work, even with high school kids, if the reward is something they really want. (Financial rewards are great incentives.)

My son hangs out with a crowd of boys who think it isn't "cool" to study hard and get good grades, so he doesn't try very hard in school. How can I convince him that being a good student can lead to a better adult life?

You can't. You can tell your son that you want him to behave in a certain way because you believe it's important and will help him in the long run. You can try to motivate change with a contract. But, whatever you do, don't use your son's friends as an excuse for his lack of effort. Don't model the idea of blaming someone else.

My child is doing only about half of the assigned homework. Should I think about punishments (or curtailing privileges) until he works harder?

At best, punishments promote a superficial compliance. But an underlying oppositional attitude, an underlying defiance, tends to grow. The parents are then forced to resort to increasingly severe punishments or deprivations. It is not a good path. Instead, try the positive incentive of a contract.

If your child did homework in the past for other teachers, perhaps the source of the problem lies with the teacher. A Department of Education paper called "What Works: Research about Teaching and Learning" makes these excellent points: "When teachers prepare written instructions and discuss home-work assignments with students, they find their students take the homework more seriously than if the assignments are simply announced. Students are more willing to do homework when they believe it is useful, when teachers treat it as an integral part of instruction, when it is evaluated by the teacher, and when it counts as part of the grade." Although parents and kids cannot expect teachers to correct every single word or problem written for homework, students need to know that their homework efforts are being noticed and affect academic achievement.

I just found out that my son has been copying most of his math homework from his best friend. Should I punish my son?

Should I tell the teacher?

A child who is copying the homework is at least not ignoring it. Evidently your son wants to turn in correct, completed work and please his teacher. Labeling a child a cheater will not help him become more honest. He shouldn't be punished. Nor should his inappropriate behavior be denied, whitewashed, or excused. Discuss with your child the reasons for his copying. Does he know how to do the work independently? Is he too overwhelmed by other activities to find the time to do it? Does he realize how the homework can help him? Does he understand that copying teaches him nothing? Seek solutions to the difficulties causing the cheating. If this doesn't work, then, yes, discuss the matter with his teacher.

My daughter, a high school sophomore, has become so busy with extracurricular activities that her grades have gone down. Should I insist that she eliminate some or all of these activities?

Your daughter has a lot of interests and is eager to develop her abilities. Don't throw cold water on her enthusiasm. Don't burden her with additional stress by making participation in the school play dependent upon a specific grade average. Remember that grades are not the only indicators of what students are learning and achieving. Students develop invaluable specific skills and generally useful "people" skills through their experiences in school athletics, publications, government, debate, and so on. In his book *Schools of Hope*, Douglas Heath says the following: "Several longitudinal studies agree that involvement in a school's cocurricular activities is the most valid school-related predictor of adult effectiveness." He quotes research that says that (comparing the contribution of grades, aptitude test scores, and other interests) youngsters who had many hobbies and jobs or who were involved in extracurricular activities were the ones most likely to succeed in later life. So our advice is to be supportive of your daughter's extracurricular interests. Ease up on her at-home responsibilities, if possible, to give her more breathing time. Help her work out a schedule that allows her to handle her hectic life more effectively.

Special Needs

We believe that parents of children with special needs should be advocates for their children (and, as their children get older, teach them to be self-advocates) so that these students have access to the special resources they are entitled to. Parents can become better educated about their children's rights and be more effective advocates by joining state and national organizations that focus on these needs. (See our list of these organizations in the Appendix.) All schools (preschool through college) that receive federal funds must provide special assistance for students diagnosed with special needs. Parents might want to consult the website Edlaw (http://www.edlaw.net), which provides information about the Individuals with Disabilities Education Act (IDEA) and the legal rights of disabled students.

My son's teacher says that Joel is very talkative and restless in class. Does that mean he has ADHD?

First, let's define our terms. ADHD stands for *attention deficit hyperactivity disorder*. When hyperactivity is not present, the condition is commonly referred to as *attention deficit disorder* (ADD). These are neurobiological disabilities that affect between 5 and 10 percent of the population.

The main symptoms of ADHD are inattention, impulsivity, and hyperactivity. These are typical inattentive behaviors: failure to listen to and follow directions, carelessness, organizational difficulties, forgetfulness, being easily distracted from the task at hand, and failure to complete tasks. A lack of impulse control may lead children to blurt out answers before being called on or to interrupt or intrude upon others in conversation or play. Hyperactive children fidget in their seats, have difficulty remaining seated, and talk or move around excessively.

Of course, many normal children also exhibit these behaviors from time to time. Moreover, these same symptoms may be due to emotional problems. When do these symptoms add up to ADHD? ADHD should be suspected if these behaviors occur frequently, in more than one setting (for example, both in school and at home), over a long period of time, and in extremely inappropriate situations. When a parent and teacher compare notes on a child's behavior and suspect ADHD, a neurologist should be consulted for a medical evaluation. Medication is sometimes prescribed, but we feel that behavior modification techniques should be tried first, since medication may have adverse side effects and/or lead to psychological dependency.

Parental attitudes toward ADHD children are important. Because they require more organizational structure than other children, ADHD children tend to draw parents into a constant relationship with them. By helping them too much, parents can make these children feel less competent than they actually are. But too little help may leave them floundering. Parents must keep reevaluating the amount of help needed and try to guide these children toward becoming more self-sufficient.

Just what is a learning disability? Does it mean that a person has a low IQ?

Not at all. In fact, Albert Einstein had a learning disability that sometimes made it difficult for him to find his way home, and Nelson Rockefeller, former governor of New York, had a reading disability. The following is a standard definition of the learning disabled person: An individual with a learning disability exhibits a significant discrepancy between potential and performance in one or more of the following areas: reasoning, oral language, reading, writing, math, or nonverbal functioning. This discrepancy is presumed to be due to central nervous system dysfunction, not primarily from mental retardation, emotional disturbance, cultural differences, experiential deprivation, or sensory impairment. The National Institutes of Health estimate that about 15 percent of Americans have some sort of learning disability. Other sources give even higher figures.

Learning disabled (LD) children may do very well in some areas but poorly in others. For example, they may retain well what is seen or read but not what is heard (or vice versa). The most common type of learning disability—dyslexia—creates problems with reading. Letters and words get confused (for example, *b* and *d* or *was* and *saw*). When, because of ongoing academic difficulties that haven't been remedied by additional help, a parent suspects that a child has a learning disability, the first step is to discuss the matter with the teacher and other school personnel. The next step is to have an evaluation conducted by a learning disability specialist. Evaluations of this type are available at schools, hospitals, and social service agencies. If a learning disability is found, the parent should take the advice of experts regarding how much and what kind of help to provide. If tutoring is suggested, parents should select a recommended tutor or institution, not just respond to an advertisement.

When LD symptoms become apparent, parents should not look the other way. The earlier a learning disability is diagnosed, the better. Often it's a relief for children to discover that they have learning disabilities, and that their academic problems are not due to being "dumb." Dr. Mel Levine, professor of pediatrics at the University of North Carolina and a renowned LD and ADHD expert, says, "Once these kids understand what the problem is, it's amazing what they can do to compensate."

Do some children have both LD and ADHD?
Yes. Estimates regarding the amount of overlap vary. In *What's Wrong With Me? Learning Disabilities at Home and School*, Regina Cicci mentions one estimate which says that of children and adolescents with learning disabilities, 20–25 percent also have ADHD, and 50–80 percent of children and adolescents with ADHD also have learning disabilities. However, these are two different problems requiring different kinds of intervention.

Our school district is starting a gifted program. What does it mean to say that a child is "gifted"? Is there anything a parent can do to get a child into such a program?
According to the federal government, gifted students are those "who give evidence of high performance capability in areas such as intellectual, creative, artistic, or leadership capacity, or in specific academic fields, and who require services or activities not

ordinarily provided by the school in order to fully develop such capabilities." The National Association for Gifted Children (NAGC) identifies these areas of giftedness: general intellectual ability, specific academic ability, creative thinking, leadership, and visual/performing arts. According to NAGC, about 5 percent of the student population—some three million children in the United States—are gifted. Although the federal government supports the idea of special services for gifted students, no federal money is provided to operate gifted programs in schools. Thus, it is left to states or individual school districts to identify and provide for gifted kids. At this time thirty-four states have a mandate to provide such services. Criteria for these programs vary, depending upon what type of gifted child the program is designed to serve. A gifted program for creative children will, of course, select a different group from a program for mathematically talented youngsters. Parents have to assume that the school can make intelligent decisions about which students "belong" in these programs.

As many parents have discovered, the gifted label doesn't always stick. A change in a child's standardized test scores or a move to a different school might cause a youngster to become "ungifted" (not reselected as part of the top 3–5 percent). If this happens to your child, don't fight the decision or express concern about what your child will be missing. There are opportunities to learn everywhere.

What kinds of homework problems, if any, do gifted students have?

Not much different from other children. For example, any student can be overly perfectionistic or passive resistant. These problems are not related to intelligence. Gifted kids may also find themselves overworked and overwhelmed by adults who are pushing them too hard. Enrichment programs, although they mean additional homework, are not often a great problem. But programs designed to accelerate students (especially in math) may be quite challenging and even frustrating. It's important for kids and parents to realize that participation in a gifted program is optional. There's no shame in quitting a program if it is making a child's life miserable. No law says a child must advance academically as fast as she possibly can.

TV, Computers, and Calculators

TV or not TV? Many parents worry that TV, that benevolent babysitter, is really an enemy in disguise, a killer of academic achievement. These are some TV questions we've received and the answers we've given:

Should kids be allowed to do homework while watching TV?
No. Background music helps some kids concentrate, but TV is too distracting.

Should there be a TV set in a child's bedroom?
No. A recent study of three hundred middle school children confirmed what you might expect: kids with TV sets in their bedrooms tend to watch more than those with TVs in other parts of their homes. And excess TV does not help a child to excel.

Should kids have a TV limit (for example, one hour per day or fifteen hours per week)? If so, what should the limit be?
A study funded by the U.S. Education Department concluded that kids who watch up to ten hours of TV per week tend to do better in school, but when the number of hours exceeds ten, school performance declines. Ten to twelve hours of TV per week is probably a reasonable limit. Via a contract or some other method, it's a good idea to limit TV viewing if you have determined that your kids are watching too much.

Some families limit TV by "issuing" half-hour TV tickets. When the child has used up his 20–24 tickets for the week, no more TV. Kids might "earn" additional TV viewing time by watching educational shows their parents want them to see or by doing something else parents request (such as more and better homework).

Other families curb TV viewing by designating one evening a week as no-TV night, or by allowing TV viewing on weekends only. No parent wants to be turned into a TV policeperson, constantly on guard overseeing what and how much the kids are watching. The best way to combat TV addiction is to help kids develop other interests, including voluntary (nonassigned) reading.

Should I buy my elementary school student a computer? At what age? What kind of computer?

A child can become computer literate and a regular computer user even if there isn't a computer at home, but a personal computer (PC) in the home can certainly enhance learning. Even preschoolers enjoy and learn from computers. One school computer consultant we know suggested a good starting age is five years old.

If you're planning to buy a computer for your child's use, it's a good idea to talk to your school's computer consultant and find out what kind of computer and word processing your child will be using at school. It may be a good idea to buy the same type of equipment for your home. Get keyboarding software so kids can graduate from the "hunt and peck" stage as soon as possible. Look for a program that has simple directions and a clear correlation between what's shown on the screen and the child's hand placement on the keyboard. Demonstration software is available from manufacturers. Try it before you buy it.

When my daughter is in her room working on her computer, I never know if she's doing homework, playing a game, or visiting an Internet site she shouldn't be visiting. How can parents be sure that the computer is being used in academically beneficial ways?

There are devices for limiting where a user can go on the Internet. You can keep your youngster from traveling to inappropriate sites, but you cannot prevent her from wasting time on-line.

The main questions to ask are these: Is she getting done the other things she's supposed to do (homework, household responsibilities, reading, exercise, socializing, etc.)? Is she spending excessive time alone with the computer? If the answers are "Yes" and "No," then no adult intervention is needed. If there's a computer problem, as with TV it may be necessary to work out a contract that places a time limit on nonacademic computer usage. If the computer is not behind a closed door in a child's bedroom, it's easier to keep an eye on what it's being used for. Also, if family members share a computer, there's less opportunity for kids to develop an addiction. With a schedule that's fair and convenient for all, sharing is possible.

Should my third grader have a calculator? Will it keep him from learning his math facts?

The emphasis in math today is on problem solving, not on memorizing. However, children are still expected to learn their addition, subtraction, multiplication, and division facts. The calculator can be used to drill on them. There's no reason it should be a hindrance. The teacher can always say, "Put the calculators away."

Learning and Teaching

How can I instill in my child a love of learning?

Love of learning is a child's most powerful ally when facing the complex and varied demands of present-day school life. This love is often derived from an original love of the parent or teacher who helps the child learn. If such parents and teachers themselves love to learn, the child naturally comes to identify with this wonderful aspect of the adults. One important factor in the development of love of learning is the pleasure a child derives when parents express admiration of the child's accomplishments. Parental praise inspires kids to try harder. But don't fake it. Praising everything a child does destroys the parent's credibility.

How early should parents begin teaching children about letters and numbers? I have three-year-old twin boys. Should I be teaching them to count and to write (or at least recognize) letters?

Teaching and learning are two different things. You may try to teach your three-year-olds anything you want. They won't learn it until they are ready. If you expose them to numbers and letters in ways that are fun for all of you, that's fine. However, there's no advantage in struggling to make your twins early readers. Being an early decoder of written symbols doesn't seem to correlate with later academic success, so there's not much point in struggling to teach a preschooler to read. Some children make the decision to become early readers. Four-year-old Marcia used to greet her mother at the door, books in hand, and say emphatically, "It's time for my reading lesson." But most are willing to wait until first grade, and that's soon enough.

This seems an appropriate place to make our plug for play—the most important activity of early childhood. It is from play that children gain a sense of their identity, the roles that others have in their lives, and even a sense of the world as a whole and how it works. In addition, play is the original source and first example of an activity that is intrinsically motivated, with rewards and satisfactions found only in the activity itself. Though young children do learn a great deal from play, academic learning is more than play; it involves taking on a certain discipline and maintaining specific goals. Given the extraordinary importance of play for all children, we would say that homework and other kinds of schoolwork have a secondary role in children's education until approximately first grade. Further, any seeming advantage children may gain from being taught various skills and abilities at an early age, with extrinsic rewards given and extrinsic criteria used to judge achievement, always runs the risk of undermining their intrinsic interest in learning. The risk is especially great when the knowledge is imposed upon the child. Moreover, such early gains are usually temporary; other children catch up in time.

I often hear the word *mentoring* used in relation to learning. How does mentoring differ from teaching? Why has it become so popular?

The word *mentor* probably comes from Homer's epic *The Odyssey*. Before Ulysses (Odysseus) embarked upon his long journey, he selected his friend Mentor to guard, guide, and teach his son Telemachus. Today the term is used to mean a wise and trusted counselor, a role model, a person who sets an example for or guides someone less experienced in a particular activity. A good teacher may be a mentor; a mentor may or may not teach what she does. Children may find mentors among older siblings or other relatives, among classmates or older students at their school, or among adults who work with them in academic or extracurricular settings. A defiant child whose relationships with the adults in his world are rocky may especially benefit from having another child as a mentor. The mentor, who is not an authority figure, sets an example of the ideal child in this particular area of work. When the mentor genuinely enjoys the mentoring relationship, this positive experience can be a true inspiration to an underachieving child.

Some school programs help students find adult mentors in occupational fields that the students have an interest in. These kinds of mentors can help young people get a sense of what it might be like to work in a particular field, thus helping them to select a career path.

We know that mentors also gain a great deal from this giving experience. Even at-risk students (those having academic difficulties in their own grades) can be good mentors for younger children and can benefit greatly, gaining knowledge plus more positive attitudes toward themselves and toward academics.

Mentoring is such a popular concept these days that it has its own newsletter, *Mentor*, published quarterly, which seeks to "re-create community through the art and practice of mentoring." (For further information about this newsletter, write P.O. Box 4382, Overland Park, KS 66204.) There is also a mentoring pro-

gram for parents who want parenting tips from older, more experienced parents who have had special training in self-esteem,
guidance, discipline, and money management. To learn more
about ParentShare, contact family studies professor Charles A.
Smith (School of Family Studies and Human Services, Justin
Hall #343, Kansas State University, Manhattan, KS 66506).

**Do you think elementary schools should eliminate grades? Do
they motivate learning or simply discourage those who get
lower grades? Are there better ways to reward effort and evaluate achievement?**

We believe that kids would be better off not getting grades until
about junior high school. In grades 1–6 there is nothing gained
by comparing students with each other. For younger children
academic competition does not encourage learning; it only dis-
courages the less able students. The aim of the elementary school
teacher is to have all children progress toward identified goals.
Written reports to parents can indicate the extent of that
progress. As children get older, comparative evaluations enter
their lives in other spheres—for example, in athletics. In older
children's games there are clear winners and losers. Grades provide one opportunity for adults to be involved in the evaluation
of kids so that youngsters are not just "stuck" with the evaluations of other children by which to measure their own worth.

**Who is responsible for seeing that kids do homework—parents
or teachers? Can't teachers and schools also provide some
incentives for homework completion?**

Absolutely. Our Appendix contains a list of suggestions regarding homework help that can be provided by teachers and
schools. Parents can encourage the implementation of some of
these ideas. Schools need to get more involved in meeting kids'
needs for homework assistance, especially in communities where
parents cannot help much with homework because of English
language problems, limited education, or very little time at home.

Family Involvement in Homework

When I look over my daughter's corrected compositions, I notice a lot of spelling and punctuation mistakes that the teacher has not corrected. Is it okay for me to point out these errors to my daughter, or will that make her lose respect for her teacher?

You can point out the mistakes if your daughter says it's okay. Ask permission first. Neither you nor your child should assume that the teacher did not correct those mistakes because he overlooked them or didn't know they were mistakes. Teachers do not correct every paper for every type of error. Often, so as not to confuse and discourage students, teachers don't correct what they haven't taught yet.

My daughter complains that school is boring and that her homework is boring. What should I do about this?

Bored, you say? Ho-hum. We've heard that song before. Your daughter is part of a very large crowd. In *Schools of Hope*, Douglas Heath writes: "Fifty-six percent of college bound public high school seniors believe that school is boring." A *Wall Street Journal* article (July 23, 1997) discusses a study conducted by Reed Larson, a University of Illinois psychologist who beeped four hundred students periodically to ask them if they were bored. Larson concluded that kids are bored a third of the time when they're in school and a quarter of the time when they're not.

Why all this boredom? Some say it is the inevitable outcome in classrooms that require students to be silent listeners and solitary learners. Others blame academic boredom on the high-tech, fast-paced society we live in, claiming it has led children to expect to be continuously entertained by exciting, novel, rapidly changing images. Still others consider boredom a natural, hostile reaction because children have to spend so much of their time in activities not of their own choosing. We believe that boredom is almost always an emotional issue; it almost never relates exclusively to the environment. There is also a large amount of unexpressed hostility in the statement "It's boring." (Think about the times you've felt bored. You felt angry and resentful because you were trapped in a meeting or at a party, didn't want to be there, and couldn't escape.)

When a child says that school is boring, at least 75 percent of the time the problem is not about the material being taught in the classroom. What's really going on? Complaints of boredom often relate to a dislike of the teacher. By complaining at home, the child is trying to get the parent overly involved in her school life. It is not a parent's job to see that children are entertained all the time. Parents should not get involved in trying to manage their children's moods. Is there anything parents can do to help? If the work is not challenging enough, parents can help kids see that school is not just a place for learning facts but also for learning how to be a good citizen, a contributing member of a community. Children who are finding school boring can perk things up by (1) helping others who don't catch on as easily; (2) volunteering to do more challenging projects; and (3) finding ways to do assigned tasks in more interesting ways. In other words, children can take some initiative to make their school lives more stimulating. Parents who choose to discuss the problem of boredom with the teacher must be cautious. There is no greater insult than saying or implying that someone is boring.

My daughter called me from school to say that she'd left her social studies report (due that day) at home. She wanted me to bring it to school. If I'd done that, I would have been late to work, so I told her I couldn't. Was I wrong? Did I give her the wrong message? Did I convey the idea that her schoolwork wasn't important to me?

Some kids have an annoying habit of turning their parents into their errand-persons. Parents should not accept this role. Here's our rule of thumb on these kinds of issues: once a semester it's OK to bring something to school for a forgetful child. More than that, you are probably being manipulated. Of course, you can't jeopardize your job or ignore your own important commitments in order to bring homework, gloves, or lunch to your child at school. Refusing may create a family crisis at the time. However, *not* doing what your child forgot to do will improve your child's memory immensely.

I used to help my daughter with her compositions for school. She sometimes complained, "You never like what I write." Now she refuses to show me her compositions. She's a B student in English. I'm an English teacher, so I could help her improve, but she won't let me. Should I insist on seeing her work?

Read only what your child wants you to read. Moreover, agree beforehand what you're reading it for (content? punctuation? organization?) and don't overstep the boundaries. If you want to teach your child about good writing, point out strengths in professional pieces you admire rather than pointing out flaws in your daughter's work. But do that only if she wants you to. Then she'll be ready to learn.

Keep in mind that a highly qualified, successful parent often has trouble teaching his own child in his area of expertise. It is extremely intimidating to be judged by an expert, whose expectations are bound to be incredibly high. That's why a superstar athlete is rarely a good coach. Your child's resistance to your "superstar" standards is healthy.

Should I be asking to see my son's corrected homework, graded essays, and graded tests? If I could see these papers, then I'd have a better idea what he needed help with. But my child doesn't bring them home or can't find them. Maybe he doesn't want me to see his work. Should I keep asking?

It's a good idea to encourage students to keep their corrected work. It might be helpful to give your son a file drawer with files for papers and tests in each subject area. Past work can be consulted when studying for a test. But should you be looking at the corrected work? Only if your child and/or the teacher wants you to. If you are going to look at the corrected work, remember the purpose. The goal is to be sure the student understands the corrections and knows how to avoid the same mistake next time. You may need to make a contract to set parental boundaries upon comments. A contract, you may remember, structures a parent's behavior as well as a child's. Your child may be more willing to allow you access to his bad tests if he knows the contract forbids you to scold him about them.

Just what is the parent's role regarding homework? Should I be checking to see if the homework is done? Commenting on how well it's done? Insisting that poorly done work be redone?

No, no, and no. There are exceptions, of course. For example, if your child is a chronic homework avoider or has a learning disability, you may be more involved in seeing that the work is done and done adequately. As we've said before, comments on effort are fine. Overall evaluative comments are risky since the teacher may not agree. But you're always safe in saying that you liked a particular part of a piece of work, if you really did. In our opinion, a parent's primary involvement with homework should be as a resource and a source of encouragement.

My husband and I have frequent arguments about homework help. He feels that I help our son too much. What's too much help?

It doesn't matter how you define too much help. If you're fighting about it, it isn't helping. We can't think of a better way to ruin your child's school life than by turning it into a parental battleground. You must come to agreement so that your son cannot use his schoolwork as a way of provoking a family feud or so that he doesn't get caught in the crossfire of a war he never wanted to start. Parents (and teachers) must agree and display a united front with regard to homework expectations, strategies, and rules.

One suggestion regarding helping "a lot": if the homework is a joint effort (parent and child), it's wise to let the teacher know that by writing a note to that effect or having both homework doers sign the paper. Then your son will not feel guilty about turning in Mom's work as his own, and the teacher will not be confused when she sees homework that is far better than what your child is able to do in class.

Do you think some parents sabotage the homework effort?
Yes, sadly, this does happen occasionally. Two types of parents come to mind: over-intrusive parents, who don't want their children to be able to succeed without their help; and envious parents, who don't want their children to become more successful than they themselves have been.

My daughter asks for my help and then complains that it isn't good enough or isn't what the teacher wants. How can I improve my homework skills?
Your homework skills are not the issue here. Your child is trying to humiliate you, and you should not allow it. Of course, children have the right (and the need) to their own private thoughts about how foolish their parents are. If we want children to function independently, we must allow them that. But when they speak to their parents, it should be with respect.

My daughter complains that her teacher gives terrible homework assignments. What is bad homework? Can a parent do anything if the assignments are really bad?
In the category of bad homework, we would place the following: busy work that doesn't teach anything useful, too much of the same thing, poorly explained assignments, work that's too hard, or work that's too easy for that academic level. Even a good teacher sometimes assigns bad homework. If your daughter complains that her homework is boring or stupid or impossible, don't try to change how she feels about it. Don't invalidate your daughter's intuition by saying something like, "You really don't think it's so bad." Yes, she does! Allow her to trust her own beliefs. You may agree or disagree that a particular assignment is pointless, unclear, or whatever. Be honest about your reaction. Although it's best to support what the teacher asks your child to do, you will

lose credibility with your child if you always defend the teacher at the expense of honesty. Every difficulty has a learning potential. Dealing efficiently and effectively with a bad assignment can teach your child something. Avoid working up a lot of anger about bad assignments; encourage an understanding attitude, a realization that everyone makes mistakes in this imperfect world.

Should I let my older son help his younger brother with homework? Are there any dangers in sibling tutoring?

This is probably not something you want to encourage on a regular basis. Your older son should not have the pressure of being responsible for his brother's academic success. However, in a pinch, sibling tutoring may work out. Here are the questions to ask yourself: Does the younger boy want to work with his older brother? Will the older brother be clear, correct, and encouraging? If he's likely to get annoyed when his little brother doesn't catch on, then obviously your younger son needs another tutor. Before letting your older son embark on tutoring, you might invite him to read our tutoring tips in Chapter 6. (Note: in families where the parents are unavailable or unable to tutor, the task may, of necessity, fall to older siblings, and many do an excellent job of it.)

Regarding homework, what is the biggest mistake a parent can make?

Doing the homework for the child. The second biggest mistake is excessive worrying about mistakes. All parents make errors regarding all aspects of parenting, including homework. Occasional, well-intentioned mistakes will not scar your child. Forgive yourself and improve.

Can you give us, in a nutshell, the most important rules for being good homework parents?

Rule 1: Listen to your intuition and not your frustration. Don't act out of anger.

Rule 2: Take your cue from the child. Unwanted help will not help!

Rule 3: Take your cue from the teacher. If it ain't broke, don't fix it.

Parents have a need to be needed. However, kids, as they mature, need to need less parenting. The greatest gift we can give our children is the confidence that they can successfully handle their own lives. We move them toward independence by gradually giving them more responsibility and autonomy. Homework is an ideal place to start.

APPENDIX

Additional Help and Resources

Homework Help Websites

This list was compiled by Sylvia and Joe Accardi of Accardi Associates Internet Training.

Alphabet Superhighway
http://www.ash.udel.edu/ash/
An extensive resource for students, teachers, and parents.

Ask a Librarian
http://www.indiana.edu/~slizzard/asciiPWP/ask_a_librarian.html
Type in a question including an E-mail address or phone number and receive an answer in less than twenty-four hours.

Ask an Expert
http//www.askanexpert.com/askanexpert/
A directory of more than three hundred websites and E-mail addresses of volunteer experts, who can answer questions and provide information on a variety of subjects.

Ask Dr. Math
http://forum.swarthmore.edu/dr.math/
A question and answer service for K–12 math students and teachers.

B.J. Pinchbeck's Homework Helper
http://tristate.pgh.net/~pinch13/
Developed by a ten-year-old boy and his dad, this site contains links
to more than four hundred sites for math and science, social studies, foreign language, music, art, etc.

Cyberspace Middle School
http://www.scri.fsu.edu/~dennis/CMS.html
A virtual school designed for 6th through 9th grade students needing curricular help with math and science. Also includes special section on science fair projects.

Homework Heaven
http://www.homeworkheaven.com
A subject directory of resources for K–12 and college students.

Internet Public Library Teen Division
http://www.ipl.org/teen/
Real teenagers and a real librarian select fun and useful sites from the
Web.

Internet Public Library Youth Division
http://www.ipl.org/youth/
A virtual public library youth room with interesting and useful websites.

Kathy Schrock's Guide for Educators
http://www.capecod.net/schrockguide/
Among the finest sites available for students and teachers. Well organized and comprehensive.

Kid Info Homework Helper
http://www.kidinfo.com/
Created to expedite the process of completing homework and classroom research assignments with a list of useful sites arranged by subject. Also links to teacher and parent resources.

Kids Connect
http://www.ala.org/ICONN/kidsconn.html
A question-and-answer-based help and referral service for K–12 students.

Looney Bin
http://www.geocities.com/Athens/3843/
A practical guide to improving study habits, writing reports, and passing tests, among other things.

Route 6-16 Homework Help Area
http://www.handiware.com/616/workhw.htm
Links to the Virtual Reference Desk, the Measurements Converter, Ask the Astronomer, and more.

Schoolwork.ugh!
http://www.schoolwork.org/
Sponsored by the Library Association of Rockland County, New York, with the idea of helping students find resources to get homework done.

Study Web
http://www.studyweb.com/
Numerous categories designed for student researchers.

Three Rivers Free Net Homework Help
http://192.204.3.5/Education/K12/homework/
Links arranged by category. Includes its own search engine for links within its databases.

Sylvia Accardi, Library Media Director at Old Orchard High
School in Skokie, Illinois, and her husband, Joe Accardi, Associate
University Librarian at Northeastern Illinois University in Chicago,
conduct Internet workshops for parents and students. For further
information, contact them at Accardi Associates Internet Training,
P.O. Box 124, Northbrook, IL 60065-0124; (847) 509-0722.

Improving Homework:
What Schools Can Do

There are many ways to provide the assistance and the inspiration kids need to do better homework. Parents can help classroom teachers and schools by coming up with positive suggestions and when necessary, supplying the man (or woman) power needed to staff homework help facilities. Here is a potpourri of ideas that can be recommended. While it may seem intrusive for an individual parent to tell a teacher or principal what to do, ideas for improving homework help can come from a PTA committee or other parent group.

Suggestions for
Classroom Teachers

- At your fall parent meeting tell parents about your homework policies and methods. Explain how much homework you'll be assigning and approximately how often. (Roughly, how much time should it take each night?) Tell parents what kinds of assignments you want them to be involved in and which you want your students to do independently.
- When a homework assignment involves using a new skill, begin the work in class to be sure students understand how to do it. (Getting started in class also helps overcome inertia; once started, it's easier to continue at home.)
- Post daily homework assignments on E-mail so computerized kids who were absent can find out what to do.
- Consider giving students your E-mail address in case important homework questions come up (especially before a big test or over a weekend).
- Use homework passes (permission to skip a homework assignment) as rewards for work well done (a high grade on a test, an outstanding project, etc.).
- If your students have more than one teacher assigning homework to them, work out an arrangement with the other

teacher(s) so that not every teacher is assigning time-consuming, difficult homework on the same day or in the same week. Spread out major projects throughout the school year.

- Consider a night off a week and at least one weekend off per month so kids get a homework break and can plan other activities for those "free" times.
- Consider making tutoring available—before school, at lunchtime, or after school—utilizing older students, parent volunteers, teacher assistants, or peer collaboration.
- Start a "Homework Anxiety Club" to give students who worry too much an opportunity to share strategies for dealing with homework stress and test anxiety.
- Consider using more interdisciplinary homework assignments. These pique the imagination and can turn homework into home fun. Themes that cross disciplines, such as dealing with change or recognizing the many faces of oppression, encourage creative responses that are exciting to develop and share.
- Consider assigning some interactive homework—activities that a student does with a parent or other adult caregiver.
- Consider voluntary homework assignments for extra credit. They're a good way to meet individual needs, providing more practice for slower learners and more challenge for advanced students.
- Try these three ways of keeping families informed about classroom activities, accomplishments, and problems: (1) once a month or so, have your students write a "Dear Mom" letter, telling the family what's new and exciting in their classroom; (2) use a "Good News from School" message form to write a quick note telling parents when a student does something good in school ("Sandy made some great drawings for our classroom bulletin board!"); or (3) use a "Home Alert" message to tell parents about a school problem. ("No math homework from Jerry this week!")
- Tell parents when you are available to take phone calls from them and how they can leave messages for you.

Suggestions for
School Administrators

- If your school or school district does not already have a home-work policy, encourage the development of one. It should give teachers and parents a clear sense of the goals of homework and the amount of homework at various grades and in various subjects. It should also discuss the school's policy regarding homework adjustments for children with learning disabilities or other special problems.

- If your school does not have a learning center, consider opening one. It can be staffed by school personnel plus volunteer parents and older students. It can provide one-on-one tutoring and computers. It might be created in a section of the school library so that reference materials would be available. If it is open after school, on week nights, and on Saturday mornings, it can be a great service for students who can't get adequate homework help at home. In communities where parents are less able to provide homework help, schools need to be more resourceful about providing it.

- Does your school have a telephone or computer homework helpline? Perhaps faculty and parents would volunteer to staff one for a few hours each evening, giving children an adult to turn to when they're "stuck."

- Help your students learn about a wide range of careers and about the educational background needed to enter these careers. On a regular basis, bring adults into the school to talk to students about occupations. Volunteers can be found by contacting parents and grandparents of your student body, local businesses, local institutions such as museums, zoos, hospitals, local speakers' bureaus, and so on. Programs like these can help children set occupational goals that will motivate more serious study habits.

- For students who are interested, match up kids with specific occupational interests and adult mentors who can provide a look at the working life of someone in that field and advice about getting into that occupation. Students can be motivated to study if they see that the effort can lead to a goal they want to achieve.

- Try a homework workshop—a get-together for parents and teachers to exchange ideas and answer each other's questions.
- Have your school librarian research instructional videos, such as *School House Rock*, and develop (or expand) your school's collection of these materials. Make them available for kids to watch at school and to borrow for home viewing.

Summer Read-Aloud Book List

Junior Kindergarten and Senior Kindergarten

Make Way for Ducklings, by Robert McCloskey
Miss Nelson is Missing, by Harry Allard
Alexander and the Terrible, Horrible, No Good, Very Bad Day, by Judith Viorst
When We Were Very Young, by A.A. Milne
Now We Are Six, by A.A. Milne
Anno's Counting Book, by Mitsumasa Anno
The Three Bears and 15 Other Stories, by Anne Rockwell
Puss in Boots and Other Stories, by Anne Rockwell
Dragon stories, by Ruth Stiles Gannett:
    My Father's Dragon
    Elmer and the Dragon
    The Dragons of Blueland

Senior Kindergarten and First Grade

Belinda's Hurricane, by Elizabeth Winthrop
Ira Sleeps Over, by Bernard Waber
Brave Irene, by William Steig
The Story of Ferdinand, by Munro Leaf
Miss Rumphius, by Barbara Cooney
Sam Bangs and Moonshine, by Evaline Ness
A Child's Garden of Verses, by Robert Louis Stevenson

First and Second Grades

The Stories Julian Tells, by Ann Cameron
Stone Fox, by John Gardiner
Amos and Boris, by William Steig
Catwings, by Ursula LeGuin
Owls in the Family, by Farley Mowat
The Littles, by John Peterson

Honey, I Love, by Eloise Greenfield
Sing a Song of Popcorn: Every Child's Book of Poems, selected by Beatrice
de Regniers

Second and Third Grades

The Velveteen Rabbit, by Margery Williams
Bunnicula, by James and Deborah Howe
The Teddy Bear Tree, by Barbara Dillon
The Chocolate Touch, by Patrick Catling
The New Kid on the Block, by Jack Prelutsky
The Wizard of Oz, by Frank Baum
The Hundred Penny Box, by Sharon Bell Mathis

Third and Fourth Grades

The Reluctant Dragon, by Kenneth Grahame
Misty of Chincoteague, by Marguerite Henry
Norse Gods and Giants, by Ingri and Edgar Parin D'Aulaire
Where the Sidewalk Ends, by Shel Silverstein
Danny, Champion of the World, by Roald Dahl
The Gold Cadillac, by Mildred D. Taylor

Fourth and Fifth Grades

Caddie Woodlawn, by Carol Ryrie Brink
The Search for Delicious, by Natalie Babbitt
The 13 Clocks, by James Thurber
Over Sea, Under Stone, by Susan Cooper
Random House Book of Poetry for Children, by Jack Prelutsky
Uncle Remus tales, by Julius Lester:
  The Tales of Uncle Remus
  The Further Tales of Uncle Remus
  More Tales of Uncle Remus
  Last Tales of Uncle Remus

Source: Francis W. Parker School, 330 W. Webster, Chicago, IL 60614.

Resources for Parents

General Interest

National PTA
330 N. Wabash Avenue, Suite 2100
Chicago, IL 60611-3604
(312) 787-0972
http://www.pta.org

National Institute of Child Health and Human Development
31 Center Drive
Building 31
Bethesda, MD 20892-2425
(301) 402-2242
http://www.nih.gov/nichd

Educational Resources Information Center (ERIC) Clearing House
on Disabilities and Gifted Education
1920 Association Drive
Reston, VA 20191-1589
(800) 328-0272
http://www.cec.sped.org/ericec.htm

Special Needs

National Association for Gifted Children (NAGC)
1707 L Street NW
Suite 550
Washington, DC 20036
(202) 785-4268
http://www.nagc.org

Children and Adults with Attention Deficit Disorders (CHADD)
499 NW 70th Avenue, Suite 101
Plantation, FL 33317
(800) 233-4050
http://www.chadd.org

Learning Disabilities Association of America (LDA)
4156 Library Road
Pittsburgh, PA 15234-1349
(412) 341-1515
http://www.ldanatl.org

National Information Center for Children and Youth with
Disabilities (NICHCY)
P.O. Box 1492
Washington, DC 20013-1492
(800) 695-0285
http://www.nichcy.org

Federation for Children with Special Needs
95 Berkeley Street
Suite 104
Boston, MA 02116
(617) 482-2915
http://www.fcsn.org

National Center for Learning Disabilities
381 Park Avenue South
Suite 1401
New York, NY 10016
(888) 575-7373
http://www.ncld.org

Parents' and Educators' Resource Center (PERC)
(Serving people with learning differences in the San Francisco Bay
area)
Charles and Helen Schwab Foundation
1660 S. Amphlett Boulevard
Suite 200
San Mateo, CA 94402-2508
(650) 655-2410
http://www.perc-schwabfdn.org

International Dyslexia Association (Formerly Orton Dyslexia
Society)
8600 LaSalle Road
Chester Building
Suite 382
Baltimore, MD 21286-2044
(410) 296-0232
http://www.interdys.org

Office of Special Education and Rehabilitative Services (OSERS)
U.S. Department of Education
330 C Street SW
Suite 3006
Switzer Building
Washington, DC 20202-2500
(202) 205-5465
http://www.ed.gov

Bibliography

Abbott, John. *Learning Makes Sense*. Hertfordshire, U.K.: Education 2000, 1994.

Berk, Laura E. and Adam Winsler. *Scaffolding Children's Learning: Vygotsky and Early Childhood Education*. Washington, DC: National Association for the Education of Young Children, 1995.

"The Best National Parks: Ratings from 40,000 readers." *Consumer Reports*. June 1997.

Bloomquist, Michael L. *Skills Training for Children with Behavior Disorders: A Parent and Therapist Guidebook*. New York: The Guilford Press, 1996.

Bradley, Bill. "Help America's Children." *Parade*. August 3, 1997.

Bryan, Janis and Carol Nelson. "Doing Homework: Perspectives of Elementary and Junior High School Students." *Journal of Learning Disabilities*. October 1994.

Burns, Marilyn. *Math: Facing an American Phobia*. Reading, MA: Math Solutions Publications (Distributed by Addison Wesley Longman), 1998.

Burns, Marilyn. *Math for Smarty Pants*. Boston: Little, Brown and Company, 1982.

Caine, Renate and Geoffrey Caine. *Making Connections: Teaching and the Human Brain*. Reading, MA: Innovative Learning Publications, Addison Wesley Publishing Company, 1991.

Cicci, Regina. *"What's Wrong with Me?" Learning Disabilities at Home and School*. Baltimore: York Press, Inc. (Timonium), 1995.

Clinton, William. *State of the Union Address*. January 23, 1996.

Cooper, Harris, et al. "Relationships Between Attitudes about Homework, the Amount of Homework Assigned and Completed, and Student Achievement." *Journal of Educational Psychology*. March 1998.

Cooper, Harris. *The Battle Over Homework*. Thousand Oaks, CA: Corwin Press, Inc., 1994.

Fintushel, Noelle. "Everyday Rituals." *Parents*. August, 1997.

"From Mazes to Millipedes: 5 Museums for Young Minds." *New York Times*. June 29, 1997.

Gardner, Howard. *Extraordinary Minds: Portraits of Exceptional Individuals and an Examination of Our Extraordinariness*. New York: HarperCollins, 1997.

Gardner, Howard. *Frames of Mind: The Theory of Multiple Intelligences*. New York: Harper Collins, 1983.

Goleman, Daniel. *Emotional Intelligence: Why It Can Matter More than IQ*. New York: Bantam Books, 1995.

Heath, Douglas H. *Schools of Hope: Developing Mind and Character in Today's Youth*. San Francisco, CA: Jossey-Bass Publishers, 1994.

Henderson, V.L. and C.S. Dweck. "Motivation and Achievement." *At the Threshold: The Developing Adolescent* (S.S. Feldman and G.R. Elliot, editors). Cambridge, MA: Harvard University Press, 1990.

Hirsch, E.D., Jr. *The Schools We Need and Why We Don't Have Them*. New York: Doubleday, 1996.

Hirsch, E.D., Jr. *What Your Kindergartner Needs to Know* (and additional volumes for grades one to six). New York: Doubleday, 1991–97.

"How Important Is Homework?" ACCESS ERIC. Office of Educational Research and Improvement, U.S. Department of Education, 1993.

Hughes, Robert. "The Delights of Downsizing." *Chicago Tribune*. February 4, 1996.

Kotulak, Ronald. "On the Record." *Chicago Tribune*. August 10, 1997.

Krashen, Stephen. *The Power of Reading: Insights from the Research*. Englewood, CO: Libraries Unlimited, 1993.

Kronholz, June. "It's Summertime and the Kids Are Bored. What Else Is New?" *Wall Street Journal*. July 23, 1997.

Ludmer, Larry. *The Great American Wilderness: Touring America's National Parks*. Edison, NJ: Hunter Publishing, Inc., 1993.

Morison, Kay, Ph.D. and Suzanne Brady. *Homework: Bridging the Gap*. Redmond, WA: Goodfellow Press, 1994.

"National PTA Standards for Parent/Family Involvement Program." Chicago: National PTA, 1996.

Newhouse, Elizabeth L., editor. *National Geographic Guide to America's Historic Places*. Washington, DC: The National Geographic Society, 1996.

O'Hara, Mary. *My Friend Flicka*. Garden City, NY: Junior Deluxe Editions, 1941.

Pajares, Frank. "Self-Efficacy Beliefs in Academic Settings." *Review of Educational Research*. Winter 1996.

Ratnesar, Romesh. "Teaching Feelings 101." *Time*. September 29, 1997.

Rimm, Sylvia. *Dr. Sylvia Rimm's Smart Parenting: How to Parent So Children Will Learn*. Avenal, NJ: Random House (Value Publishing), 1997.

Robinson, F.B. *Effective Study*. New York: Harper & Row, 1970.

Rowntree, D. *Learn How to Study*. New York: Harper & Row, 1983.

Ryan, Michael. "If You Can't Teach Me, Don't Criticize Me." *Parade*. May 11, 1997.

Salzman, Marian and Robert Pondiscio. *The Ultimate On-Line Homework Helper*. New York: Avon Books, 1996.

Schwartz, Lynne Sharon. *Disturbances in the Field*. New York: Harper & Row, 1983.

Shermer, Michael. *Teach Your Child Science: Making Science Fun for Both of You*. Los Angeles: Lowell House, 1995.

"Standardized Exams Get an 'A.'" *Business Week*. June 30, 1997.

Sylwester, Robert. *A Celebration of Neurons: An Educator's Guide to the Human Brain*. Alexandria, VA: Association for Supervision and Curriculum Development, 1995.

"To Your Books: Homework." *The Economist*. U.K., The Economist Newspaper Ltd. May 6, 1995.

Warton, Pamela M. "Responsibility for Homework: Children's Ideas about Self-Regulation." (Sydney, Australia: Macquarie University) U.S. Department of Education: Educational Resources Information Center (ERIC), 1993.

Washburn, Deborah Field, editor. *Fodor's '97 USA*. New York: Fodor's Travel Publications, Inc. (Random House, Inc.), 1996.

"What Works: Research about Teaching and Learning." *Condition of Education*. U.S. Department of Education: National Center for Education Statistics, 1986.

Zorn, Eric. "Without Failure, Jordan Would Be a False Idol." *Chicago Tribune*. May 19, 1997.

Index